PRAISE FOR JESSE NEWTON
AND SIMPLIFY WORK

For all those that have experienced the debilitating effects of complexity in their organization this book is for you. Simplifying work can free people to perform at their best. Jesse reveals the major drivers of organizational complexity and the steps to be taken to throw off the shackles of 20th century ways of working. A must read for those that believe in a better way of getting work done.

JON KATZENBACH, Former senior partner at McKinsey & Co, Booz & Co and Katzenbach Partners, author of ten books including *The Wisdom of Teams* and *Leading Outside the Lines*

The time is now ripe to liberate the creative and productive capacity of our people and *Simplify Work* provides the recipe. Jesse has infused design thinking to solve the challenge of debilitating complexity and with many compelling examples and stories the case for simplifying work is a very strong one. A must read for contemporary business leaders

RENETTA MCCANN, Chief People Officer, Leo Burnett. Adjunct Professor, Northwestern University

In these increasingly complex times the demand placed on business executives have never been greater. Many business leaders long for more simplified ways of working but often find it hard to get out of their own way. *Simplify Work* provides a clear approach for re-gaining clarity on those things that truly matter most and letting go of the things that get in the way. A timely book for executives looking for ways to drive a step-change in productivity, and quickly.

BRIAN COLLIE, Senior Partner,
The Boston Consulting Group

Simplify Work raises relevant questions about challenges today's organizations face and proposes intriguing new solutions. How do we focus on things that matter the most? How do we more rapidly let go of things that get in the way of effective and efficient organizational operation? The ideas, frameworks and approaches spelled out in *Simplify Work* contribute to the discourse about new ways to catalyze organizational evolution. Read the book and join the conversation!

DORIE BLESOFF, Chief People Officer, Relativity.
Adjunct Professor, Northwestern University

Simplify Work

SIMPLIFY WORK

Crushing Complexity to
Liberate Innovation,
Productivity, and Engagement

JESSE W. NEWTON

NEW YORK

LONDON • NASHVILLE • MELBOURNE • VANCOUVER

Simplify Work

Crushing Complexity to Liberate Innovation, Productivity, and Engagement

Published in New York, New York, by Morgan James Publishing. Morgan James is a trademark of Morgan James, LLC. www.MorganJamesPublishing.com

ISBN 9781642790825 paperback
ISBN 9781642790832 eBook
Library of Congress Control Number: 2018943181

Cover Design by:
Megan Dillon
megan@creativeninjadesigns.com

Interior Design by:
Chris Treccani
www.3dogcreative.net

Morgan James is a proud partner of Habitat for Humanity Peninsula and Greater Williamsburg. Partners in building since 2006.

Get involved today! Visit
MorganJamesPublishing.com/giving-back

DEDICATION

To my lovely ladies: Kelly, Isabella, and Lorelai

CONTENTS

PREFACE

t was the experience of scaling the summit of Mount
Kilimanjaro in Tanzania that spawned the idea for this
book. Sitting down in a camp in the Serengeti, days after
almost dying of altitude sickness on the way to the top of the
mountain, I felt the desire to share what I have learned on the
power of simplification. On that excruciating summit push,
the purity of focus was evident: take a step, breathe, take
another step, breathe, and so on. Without breaking down the
significant undertaking into minute actions, the task would
have seemed unachievable. Then, reflecting on how more and
more companies seem overawed with the scale and reach of
their crippling complexity, I felt the time was right to share my
experiences and research regarding how to go about simplifying
work in a careful and sustainable manner.

As a leader of a global consulting firm that specializes
in organizational simplification and an expert advisor
at Northwestern University on the topic of organization

effectiveness, I have had and continue to have many diverse encounters on the topic of simplification. It is quite evident that complexity is wreaking havoc on organizations and individuals at an increasing rate. We are on the front step of a new industrial revolution but are still using 20th-century methods of organizing how work gets done. As a result, many organizations cannot realize the phenomenal performance potential that this new revolution promises. Also, individuals are unhappy, unhealthy, and burning out at increasing rates.

As an expert in organization effectiveness, I feel saddened every time I witness individuals and teams paralyzed by controlling and energy-sapping rules, processes, and transactional expectations, all of which are now endemic in most complex global matrixes. This rising sense of hopelessness is holding our organizations back from delivering breakthrough innovations and executing at speed. The time is right to rethink how work gets done. Let's use simplification as the guiding light to regain clarity on what is truly important and set our people free.

This book is written for anyone that believes there could be a better way to run our businesses in the 21st century. If you feel frustrated with overburdening complexity or for likeminded lovers of simplicity this book is for you. It promises to reveal the typical drivers of complexity in our organizations and in our lives and provides a practical method for simplifying work. This book will deliver a newfound clarity on the case for simplification and the steps you will need to take to unleash its potential, and it will leave you feeling inspired by the liberating reality you could create in both your organization and your life.

Given that this book is on simplification, I thought it important for it to be punchy and succinct. Thus, this is not a lengthy business book that will take an extended period of time to get through. It is more suited to a long flight or a lazy long weekend. I have woven in many examples and experiences to bring to life the ideas that I introduce. I have also used a casual tone as much as possible, along with sprinkling in some personal stories to keep the read fun.

For more information on simplify work please visit www.simplifywork.com.

CHAPTER 1

Bogged Down in a Spaghetti of Structure, Process, Systems, and Rules

An epidemic is affecting businesses large and small. This epidemic is debilitating complexity. The disease restricts innovation, limits productivity, disengages the workforce, and eventually leads to organizational failure. This book provides a cure for this disease in the form of a tested method for identifying, removing, and redesigning the things that get in the way of focusing on what is most important.

Debilitating complexity takes the form of unnecessary and complicated structures, processes, systems, rules, metrics, checks and balances, and so on. Businesses traditionally add more and more of these things as they grow. There seems to be an acceptance that as a business grows, complexity and complicatedness are natural by-products. And while complexity certainly does increase as businesses mature, it does not mean that it needs to stifle innovation and entrepreneurship. The same story plays out over and over again once a company gets to a certain size: the entrepreneurial leaders decide that their juvenile business is becoming an adolescent and want to be taken seriously, so they bring in an experienced "big company" professional. The big company person then sets about installing all of the "discipline" that a serious organization requires— defined roles and responsibilities, performance metrics, committees, strict common processes, and so on, and so on. Then, all of sudden, people begin adhering to their newfound role expectations, they start to get lost in all the processes and paperwork, they become scared to step outside of their defined role, and spontaneous rich innovation becomes a distant memory.

In a recent study 74% of respondents rated their organization as complex.[1] In this digital age, when technology is fueling rapid changes in consumer preferences and reshaping industries, it is critical that companies innovate well and fast. Companies that are bogged down in slow decision making, risk intolerance, and siloed protectionism are destined to fail.

The current complexity crisis is largely due to many organizations holding on to outdated and obsolete methods of organizing how work gets done. These 20th-century approaches

---

1   Dimple Agarwal, Ardie van Berkel, and Burt Rea, "Simplification of Work: The Coming Revolution," *Deloitte Human Capital Trends Report 2015,* https://www2.deloitte.com/insights/us/en/focus/human-capital-trends/2015/work-simplification-human-capital-trends-2015.html, accessed September 11, 2017.

to organization structure and management are strangling our productive and innovative potential. They are limiting the thinking power of our people and not effectively using the resources at organizations' disposal.

From an individual perspective, how we protect and allocate our time and energy is becoming increasingly paramount. The most important resource people have is their time, and we are spending far too much of it on the wrong things. We are pulled in so many directions and have to spend so much time and energy navigating through a labyrinth of processes and structures that we have lost touch with what really matters. We simply do not have the time and energy to do our best work on the most important activities.

As we are working longer and longer on increasingly low-value work, we often don't even realize it. We have become accustomed to the four approvals we require to do anything and accustomed to going through a leader to talk to someone in a different function. We're accustomed to navigating through three separate systems to find the information we need, and we're accustomed to dedicating a quarter of the year to complete the budgeting process. Let's not forget about that report one of your leaders within the matrix needs; that clearly should take precedence over everything else.

Deep down we know something is not quite right. We are not spending quality time doing the work we were hired to do. We find that it is getting harder to stay on top of everything and enjoy a good balance or even a balance at all. This results in us simply checking out. Engagement scores across companies over the past 30 years have consistently decreased. According to Gallup, only 28% of the US workforce is engaged at work, the rest are either actively disengaged or merely not engaged.[2]

The implication for business is that things move too slow, people think and act in silos, it's hard to get anything done, decision making is poor, innovation is missing, risk-taking is low, and it all leads to increasing costs and being left behind by more nimble competitors. But it doesn't have to be this way. Advances in technology are enabling us to spend less time on low-value activities, both in business and on the personal front. With our smartphones we're able to do so much that we weren't able to do in years gone by. We can buy products, order a taxi, book a flight, keep track of your heart rate, and more. There is also the rise of the voice assistant, like Amazon's Alexa. You can leverage this for anything from automating and simplifying weekly grocery shopping to controlling your music. The challenge is that most businesses have not kept up with these developments, so many people are still stuck wasting a significant part of their day doing low value, non-core activities.

Chaotic complexity exists in many organizations, from the private sector to nonprofits and certainly in government. There are many drivers of debilitating complexity, but a common one is the added structure, process, rules, systems, and so on that come with growth. As an organization grows, new business units are created, back-office services need to expand, and more layers are added to the structure. It can become a vicious virtuous cycle. As more departments are created, cross-functional communication weakens, resulting in coordinating groups being established, thereby adding to the spaghetti of handoffs, approval processes, and committees.

---

2   "The State of the Global Workplace," Gallup Consulting, 2011, http://www. gallup.com/strategicconsulting/145535/State-Global-Workplace-2011.aspx.

A recent example of an organization that has experienced this is GoPro. This innovative camera company experienced sensational growth over a decade and had a highly successful IPO in 2014. However, between 2015 and 2017 the company lost money most quarters. Where the wheels started to fall off for GoPro was the complexity creep that the company allowed during its explosive growth. The company, influenced by its fast growth and investor expectations, decided to create new business units to tap into new industry segments and foster continued growth. At one point they were developing more than 30 series of different shows that they wanted to post on a new streaming platform that they were creating simultaneously. They also were building new products, including a drone and an underwater camera. They went from 700 employees to 1,600 employees in 18 months. Budgets increased tenfold. With this expansion, the company went from a flat simple structure to multiple siloed business units. What was once a fast-moving entrepreneurial company became a complicated, lethargic beast. The company was losing its way. The founder and CEO, Nick Woodman, recognized this: "We went from being thrifty and scrappy and efficient and wildly innovative to being bloated and—what's the opposite of thrifty? It was undermining the strength of our brand and deconstructing everything we had built." The company's newfound convoluted complexity started to come to life through serious quality control issues, which translated into production issues that scarred the company's reputation. Woodman says, "The teams were killing themselves to launch the products on time. We were doing too many things, and it was taking too long to make decisions because management was juggling too many projects at once." Woodman and his leadership team have since set about simplifying their company.

They have closed down underperforming business units, let go of more than a quarter of their employees, and gone back to a simplified flat structure that is refocused on its core business. GoPro now does a lot less, but it does these things well. Their products no longer are experiencing performance problems, and their mean video views are up 65%. There is still work to be done for GoPro to restrengthen their reputation, but with their newfound organizational clarity they are well placed to reenergize their business. Woodman distills it nicely: "We structured ourselves as a much bigger business. But complexity breeds complexity, and we learned that when the organization is structured that way, you're not as nimble. You're not as athletic. When you have fewer lines of communication, things are less likely to break or get lost in translation."[3]

Another common driver of complexity is in the acquisition and integration of other companies. Acquired organizations bring their own complexity in the form of convoluted structures, embedded ways of working, and legacy IT architecture or lack thereof. Complexity from systems in particular can be a highly potent driver of frustration, wasted time, and energy. The post-integration systems mess often leaves an acquiring organization IT department scrambling to make sense of the legacy systems, and it often takes a substantial amount of time to either connect or sunset the disparate and disconnected systems. While this significant undertaking is in process, employees have to attempt to get their work done by navigating through the various systems. This can be a major source of complexity and frustration and lead to turnover of talent.

---

3   Tom Foster, "Doubts, Fears, and Two Very Bad Years," *Inc.* 39, no. 10 (winter 2017-2018): 53-60.

The opposite can also happen: an acquired company may have better, simplified technology and have to deal with a spaghetti of disconnected systems in the acquiring company as it is integrated. I witnessed this during an integration of two major healthcare companies. The acquirer was over 100 years old, a typical slow-moving giant, and the acquired company was smaller, younger, and nimbler. The employees of the acquired company were used to working with speed, and their systems enabled it. When they were enveloped into the acquiring giant and were exposed to the disconnected systems and processes of the larger company, the vast majority of the employees, especially top talent, chose to resign within the first year. The pain of wasted time and energy getting lost in the labyrinth of programs, share points, and collaboration platforms was simply too much to handle. Internal complexity cost the acquiring company a lot of the value it had sought in the acquisition.

Companies that are mired in debilitating complexity can break free of its hold. With strong leadership support and a clear approach for attacking complexity companies can re-energize their people by bringing back the laser focus, reducing the clutter and releasing the reins on innovation. The epidemic of complexity is spreading throughout the world of business and if it is not reined in, those that have managed to keep it at bay will leap ahead and those that don't will fall by the wayside.

Fourth Industrial Revolution without the Productivity Gains

For thousands of years prior to the first industrial revolution mankind's productivity gains were made very slowly. The discovery of the wheel, and domesticating horses and cows for farm work were a couple of significant discoveries or developments that had positive impacts on productivity. However, thousands of years passed where no major advancements were made in productivity. Then around 1800 the first industrial revolution began in Britain with the invention of steam powered mechanization. All of a sudden, machines like the steam powered locomotive or production machines, blew up our dependence on human and animal power. So much more could now be done by leveraging this new technology. This first industrial revolution resulted in significant gains in global standards of living.

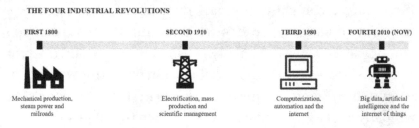

THE FOUR INDUSTRIAL REVOLUTIONS

FIRST 1800 — SECOND 1910 — THIRD 1980 — FOURTH 2010 (NOW)

Mechanical production, steam power and railroads

Electrification, mass production and scientific management

Computerization, automation and the internet

Big data, artificial intelligence and the internet of things

Figure 1.

A century ago, around 1910, and about 110 years after the first industrial revolution the second industrial revolution began. During this transformative period industry installed production lines that were powered by new electricity grids. Also during this period Frederick Taylor introduced scientific management and companies began to define processes and manage the speed of tasks. This fueled another important wave of productivity enhancements that delivered the next step-change in living standards.

Fast forward 70 years to around 1980 and enter information technology, which connected people and businesses online. Computers took over from type writers and with the discovery of faxing and then emailing the speed of business was transformed. No longer were communications limited to the speed of postal systems or telephone calls. This third industrial revolution transformed how we work once again and delivered another step-change in productivity and efficiency.

Today, we are on the front step of the fourth industrial revolution. We are living in a digital era where artificial intelligence, big data and the internet of things are revealing opportunities for us to finally step out of transactional, repeatable work and focus our time, energy and capabilities on the activities that deliver the greatest value. However, while we are in the midst of the fourth industrial revolution we have yet to realize the productivity improvements that previous revolutions delivered. Why is it that this revolution isn't delivering the performance and productivity improvement of previous revolutions? I believe a significant driver is the high degree of unnecessary complexity within our organizations that is holding us back. Fueling the propagating nature of complexity are the 20th century organization structures and management practices that many organizations are holding onto.

Many large organizations today, especially traditional industry leaders, are stuck in 20th-century ways of working. They have dense bureaucratic structures and strict, formal processes with rules and more rules. Traditional best practices told us that we need these things when we establish a new business unit, functional group, or working group of some sort. We believed that we need detailed descriptions of all roles, responsibilities, reporting relationships, decision rights, processes, and rules to get anything done. These things were needed because humans weren't to be trusted. Installing detailed strict structures meant that leaders could control the output of their people, thereby limiting the risk of mistakes and establishing a baseline of quality. So, as companies grew, they added more and more structures and gradually became complicated messes.

The lines and boxes mode of operating made sense in a time when requirements were simpler and before automation or artificial intelligence. When all a business had to do was produce a product or service that was focused on price or quality, complexity could be managed. People could come to work, do the same thing, and go home, and the company would continue to grow. Like a well-oiled machine, human capital could be managed, measured, and organized as leaders saw fit.

The challenge today is that the speed of industry evolution is so fast that people must be engaging all their intellect on the highest priorities so that companies can keep up with market developments. Also, customers are demanding more and more. They expect high quality, low cost, speed, reliability, and global consistency all at the same time. These requirements coupled with keeping pace with industry developments mean that companies cannot afford to have their people bogged down and distracted in low-value work. It is now critical to refocus teams and strip out and simplify unnecessary or low-value work. This requires rethinking how strategy is distilled, how organization structure is designed, and how processes, systems, and cultures are put in place and nurtured to fuel a new way of facilitating rich innovations and fast and accurate execution.

We are certainly in an age where companies have to deal with a lot of complexity; it is how they deal with complexity that sets them apart from their peers. Importantly, it's not just the small start-ups that have successfully built companies that control complexity and maintain focus on innovation and entrepreneurship; many large companies have successfully revived their companies through simplification.

Amazon is in the process of taking over the world. Amazon was ranked as the number one most effectively run company of 2017 as part of the Management Top 250, a business ranking that analyzes companies based on the ideals and teachings of the late Peter Drucker.[4] But Amazon had to take deliberate steps to simplify its structure to foster the high innovation that the company is now recognized for. Growing up, Amazon possessed a typical 20th-century structure that included layers of managers, bureaucracy, processes, rules, and so on. They found that the company was not delivering the creative solutions that they desired, so in the early 2000s they stripped out bureaucracy and complexity and installed an autonomous small team structure. Individuals were carefully selected to join teams that famously are no bigger than can be fed with two pizzas. Each team has autonomy to work, decide, and execute as they see fit. There are still governing bodies that ensure alignment and coordination across teams as well as test them with questions such as how much their product or service would cost, how much it will sell for, and the potential launch date. But the teams are accountable for performance and ongoing improvements. Amazon acknowledged that its number one ranking in the Management Top 250 was due in large part to their shift to an autonomous small team structure and the significant innovation this model has enabled. They have effectively bred a culture that exemplifies agility and entrepreneurship and keeps complacency in check, which, for a company as large and successful as Amazon, is no easy feat.

---

4   Vanessa Fuhrmans and Yoree Koh, "The 250 Most Effectively Managed U.S. Companies—and How They Got That Way," *Wall Street Journal*, December 6, 2017, https://www.wsj.com/articles/the-most-effectively-managed-u-s-companiesand-how-they-got-that-way-1512482887, accessed December 6, 2017.

The reality today is that simply following rules and mechanical processes will not deliver the value required to win in the marketplace. As we progress into the fourth industrial revolution, machines will increasingly be able to do any task that can be defined with clear rules, processes, and standards. The power of the internet is breaking down barriers to entry, so incumbents are increasingly being challenged by start-ups that are moving at much faster speeds. We need to free our people from the noise of low-value work and allow them to focus on what will truly have the greatest positive impact on the business. The time is ripe to introduce carefully designed simplification solutions to allow organizations to rev back up and reinfuse the focus, energy, and execution that made them originally successful. This is how we will realize the productivity potential of our current industrial revolution.

Organizational and Individual Opportunity

This is not just an organizational issue. We, individually, are also responsible for allowing complexity to drive constant distraction, low focus, and low energy. We live highly cluttered lives, have become addicted to checking our phones, are too responsive to interruptions, and do not nurture, protect, and direct our most productive energy.

We experience a constant stream of interruptions. We have phones that vibrate or ping anytime we receive a new email, a calendar invite or reminder, a LinkedIn or Facebook update, or a notification from the plethora of apps that want to keep us engaged. These disruptions break our focus and reduce our ability to think deeply. But we don't seem to mind. We are now so addicted to checking our phones every few minutes that if we are away from them for any extended period of time, we suffer withdrawal. According to one publication, we check our phones well over 100 times per day and up to every six seconds in the evening.[5]

If we're working on our computer, we have instant messaging popping up at random times breaking our focus. We have multiple programs open at the same time and seem to click back and forth between them endlessly. We have the browser open with multiple pages up at the same time. We make it too easy to get distracted and pulled from the work that matters.

We allow our calendars to be booked back to back with meetings on every topic imaginable. Our global teams demand an always-on mentality, and that's what we give them. We do not recognize when we do our best work and religiously protect this time to focus it on what matters most. And we don't let ourselves recharge our batteries when we're not doing work, thereby increasing the speed of burnout and generally limiting our potential.

In almost every one of the 100+ companies I have consulted with over the years, I have witnessed leaders simply going from one meeting to the next. It is a stream of one topic to the next without breaks. No time to reflect, process, and synthesize. No time to recharge and refocus. The highest opportunities seem to get lost in the jumble of various things that take up their time. Having to deal with so many things naturally limits the depth of thinking and focus and consequently quality of their contributions on the things that matter most.

---

5   Victoria Woollaston, "How Often Do You Check Your Phone? The Average Person Does It 110 Times a Day", *Daily Mail Online*, October 8, 2013, http://www.dailymail.co.uk/sciencetech/article-2449632/How-check-phone-The-average-person-does-110-times-DAY-6-seconds-evening.html, accessed October 17, 2017.

Many of us have simply lost touch of the work that truly delivers the greatest value and impact to the business. We stay busy on the tasks that are apparently most urgent. We are often stuck in firefighting mode, responding to problems, errors, or crises that keep us from operating in a strategically proactive manner. I remember a conversation I had with a highly experienced executive coach. I asked him how much time on average his leaders spend on reactive work, like responding to email or attending low-value meetings. He said they spend at least two-thirds of their day, with many allowing all their time to be absorbed by reactionary work. The opportunity to refocus on the highest priorities and remove or redesign how the low-value, non-core, reactionary work is managed is huge. The spike in productivity, strategic impact, and cost savings would be tremendous if habits were built around prioritization, time management, and focus.

It's interesting how hoarding low-value physical stuff also contributes to our lack of focus or highly complicated lives. This could be holding on to anything from surplus documentation to unused clothing. We pile up documents that we'll get to later when we have more time, or we keep that shirt that we sort of like but will probably never wear again. For anything that doesn't fit in our packed storage cupboards, basements, or garages, we purchase extra space in an external storage unit. What many of us don't realize is that all of this excess stuff weighs on our mind and reduces our ability to think clearly. The act of culling excess stuff is mentally liberating and one of the most crucial steps to simplifying your life and taking back control of what's important.

Another area that seems to be underappreciated is our energy. Our energy, both physical and mental, is a driver of our productivity, creativity, and problem-solving abilities. We do not do enough to nurture, protect, and dedicate our best energy toward the highest priority activities. Most of us don't even consider how to structure our day so that we best use our most productive time. We also have so much on and are pulled in so many directions that we don't take time to recharge, let go, and refocus. We work late into the night and do not prioritize our sleep. Simple shifts in how you organize and structure your day will increase energy levels, and as a result, increase not only your productivity and impact but also your general well-being and happiness. This is why topics such as mindfulness and meditation are getting more traction in mainstream business. People are discovering that taking five minutes to switch off all the noise in your prefrontal cortex is hugely beneficial as it can help to elevate thinking and reduce impulse reactions to the various fires going on around you.

There is clearly a ton of opportunity to simplify both business and our lives. The potential returns are tremendous. Ironically, getting to simple or keeping things simple is often quite challenging and certainly more difficult than adding more complexity and complications.

What If...

What if we could take a fresh look at our businesses, reconsider what is really important, and start to focus our time and energy on those things that matter. Imagine the positive effect it would have on your people if you told them they now have permission to do more of the work they were hired for. Imagine their sense of liberation if you removed a big chunk of the activities that soak up their time: low-value training, compliance, meetings that should be emails, expense processing, report building, budget setting, clunky performance management, and so on.

The time is right to simplify and focus.

Complexity exists at both organizational and individual levels. Simplifying complexity, both organizational and individual, is not easy but certainly can be done with some drive and determination.

Getting to Simple Is Not Easy

The act of simplification is not easy. It's a lot easier to add complexity than it is to design a simplified solution that delivers the desired function. It requires intelligence and perseverance to reduce something complex and messy into something streamlined, prioritized, and simple. It's much easier to add on another process, rule, or detail than it is to design something simple that strips elements away to reveal critical elements that can serve to solve the root cause of a problem, enhance focus, and/or accelerate understanding and buy-in.

Given the relative ease with which complexity takes hold, it incrementally creeps into business and propagates. It's like a vine that gradually grows up and around a tree before eventually strangling the life out of it. Simplifying work and keeping it simple takes strong desire and commitment from leadership. Leadership has to see the potential value of simplification and go after complexity with a blowtorch and a big axe. Without strong leadership commitment, any simplification effort will falter and fail, and complexity will retake the throne.

While getting to simple may take a lot of hard work and persistence, there are some core components or ways of "getting to simple" to help those in this important endeavor. Books have been written on the topic simplicity that break down how to achieve simplicity into specific elements. In his book *The Laws of Simplicity*, John Maeda introduces 10 laws or critical elements of simplicity[6]:

1. Reduce: The simplest way to achieve simplicity is through thoughtful reduction.
2. Organize: Organization makes a system of many appear fewer.
3. Time: Savings in time feel like simplicity.
4. Learn: Knowledge makes everything simpler.
5. Differences: Simplicity and complexity need each other.
6. Context: What lies in the periphery of simplicity is definitely not peripheral.
7. Emotion: More emotion is better than less.
8. Trust: In simplicity we trust.
9. Failure: Some things can never be made simple.
10. The One: Simplicity is about subtracting the obvious and adding the meaningful.

I like number 10: simplicity is about subtracting the obvious and adding the meaningful. This is a nice way of distilling how to simplify. Numbers 1 and 2 are a couple of the more important steps in simplifying. Making sense of many things or a complicated mess is done by organizing them into logical groupings. Then, based on the intent or strategy, you can determine how to prioritize those that are most important versus those that aren't. Those less important things can be removed or reduced, thereby delivering the value that simplicity promises: focus, clarity, understanding, and beauty.

---

6   John Maeda, *The Laws of Simplicity: Design, Technology, Business, Life* (Cambridge, MA: MIT Press, 2006).

My list for how to simplify looks like this:

1. Get clear on purpose
2. Organize
3. Reduce

Get Clear on Purpose

There has to be a clear sense of what the bigger picture is so you can begin to remove the things that are not as useful. Without clarity on the strategy, mission, or vision, you simply can't begin to remove or reduce the things that are cluttering the business. This is why strong corporate communication functions play such an important role within companies: the good ones are highly effective at crystalizing a company's strategy, mission, and vision via creative communications that enable people to understand what is most important. The communications capture attention and distill complex information into seemingly simple points via innovative pictures, videos, stories, and metaphors. When this is missing in companies, people lose sight of or are unsure about what is most important and are left to blindly adhere to their manager's instructions versus being able to think and act for themselves. A broader understanding of the strategic context has to be the first step in simplifying anything.

Some questions that can help you to get clear on purpose include:

- What does success look like?
- What is the best outcome we could achieve?
- What is going to deliver the greatest value?

Organize

Once a clear understanding of the strategic context has been established and key objectives are known, work can begin on organizing the chaos. A comprehensive picture of the current state, whether it be how work is done, content in a document, or possible features for a product, should be obtained. As we'll talk about in the next chapter, there are great ways of completing this current state capture using the design thinking method of putting yourself in others' shoes versus simply crunching data. When the laundry list or dump of current state information is collected, themes can be extracted and used to group and organize the minutiae. This enables sense to be made of the complexity as it creates a perception that the many have become fewer.

Some questions to help with organizing chaos include:

- What are the themes?
- Can the themes be organized by relative strategic importance?
- Is there a way of assessing the degree of ease in removing or integrating non-core components?

Reduce

Once you have the groupings or themes and you have a clear idea of what you're trying to achieve, the next intuitive step is to prioritize and reduce and remove those things that are not essential. This is a key step in simplifying, but it is also very challenging. To some people it can feel counterintuitive to remove detail, functionality, or options. It can feel like something that is comprehensive is being dumbed down. This is why not all see the value of simplicity. These individuals believe that complex solutions are more ingenious. They create highly complicated solutions to illustrate their significant intellect. As a junior consultant, I was guilty of this perspective. As a young professional out to prove myself, I thought that if I designed something highly detailed and complicated it would show my expertise and demonstrate the comprehensive approach I had taken. With more experience, I realized that the value of the design, whether it be an organization structure or process, is in how it is used by people. It quickly became apparent that the more complicated something is, the less likely it is that people will go near it. People are naturally much more drawn to something simple – something they can quickly understand and make sense of. If something takes a couple of hours of study to understand, even if it is in theory a good design, it will never take hold. I learned with experience that one the greatest skills to have is the ability to distill many things into a few. That said, there will continue to be those that veer toward the complex, so they need to continue to be met with the beautifully simple and hopefully one day they will see the light.

Antoine de Saint-Exupéry, the famous French writer, said it nicely: "Perfection is reached not when there is nothing left to add, but when there is nothing left to take away."[7]

Key questions that can be posed to help reduce something complex down its core include:

- What is most strategically important?
- What is least important and easiest to remove?
- How can non-core elements be redesigned or integrated?

---

7   Antoine de Saint-Exupery, *Airman's Odyssey* (Mariner Books, 1984).

Earlier I mentioned how simplification is often challenging given the need for something, whether it be a product or an organization, to deliver a function(s). Reducing things to make something simple often means reducing function. The key is to reveal and focus on the few most important functions. Given that large global organizations require a lot of function, the art of balancing it with simplicity can be a challenging task. Having experience and expertise in certain areas, such as organization design, strategy, culture, change management, and Lean Six Sigma helps with getting that balance just right. But there is also one other capability that is a major driving force of simplification: common sense. Having grown up in New Zealand, where there is a strong commonsense culture, I highly appreciate the value of this simple mindset. If there is a better way of doing something, let's do it. No need for playing political games or getting multiple approvals or completing boil the ocean analysis; just do it and move on. Many organizations suffer from severe risk aversion and as a result require in-depth analysis to validate every decision that is made. This ensures that everything moves at a glacial pace and takes the wind from the sails of innovation. Companies that have infused entrepreneurship into their culture know the right balance of common sense and fact-based decision making. There will always be the big decisions or projects that should be informed by fact-based analytics. These insights increasingly will be available in real-time as technology capabilities improve, but in the meantime it takes time—and often expensive strategy consultants—to crunch the numbers and produce the insights required to make the decisions. So there's a big opportunity for many organizations to leave the deep, time-consuming analysis for the big hairy projects and lean on common sense for every other decision or piece of work. Using common sense is also a great way to assess and remove the many drivers of unnecessary complications in an organization. Try asking basic questions like these:

- Do we really need a coordinating function between these two groups?
- Do we really need this report that frequently?
- Do we really need that number of approvals?
- Do I really need to attend that meeting?

Asking these basic questions and being real with the responses can reveal immediate ways to step away from unnecessary distractions and time sucks. Sometimes the best solution is the simplest one right in front of you. It makes me think of a story I heard about the Great Wall of China. Structural engineers traveled to China to investigate the Great Wall. They wanted to figure how the wall, having withstood intense heat and cold over the centuries, had retained its structural integrity in many large parts. They discovered that a secret ingredient was used in the cement. The secret ingredient was sticky rice. The ancient Chinese had discovered that adding a food they eat every day into the cement mix enabled the wall to expand in heat and contract in the cold. It was an ingenious solution from the simplest source. Indeed, sometimes the best solution is the simplest one.

Cutting through organizational complexity is not easy, but it can be done, and the potential returns can be tremendous. While there are some common helpful methods of getting to simple, such as getting clear on purpose, organizing, and reducing, there is a bigger process that more effectively guides the simplification process. We have found that leveraging a design thinking approach accelerates the process while supporting highly innovative solutions. Let's now step into the world of design.

CHAPTER 2

Using Design Thinking to Simplify Work

I agree with Tom Kelley, founder of IDEO, when he said, "design is not a thing, it's a mindset that you use to see the world."[8] Designers are inherently innovators and problem solvers who seek to simplify. They have to manage often competing pressures across technical, commercial, and human needs. At the same time they have to deal with three core constraints: feasibility, viability, and desirability. But once these pressures and constraints are met in a solution, it often creates substantial

---

8   High Resolution, "#16: IDEO's Tom Kelley Is Design Thinking's Ultimate Disciple, He Makes the Case as to Why," YouTube video, posted May 28, 2017, https://youtu.be/L1pBhHjGKvI.

value. People take for granted how their lives are shaped by design, from the physical feel of a seat to the convenience of an online shopping experience to the basic value of a windshield wiper. Design is everywhere and is constantly seeking to improve the human experience.

A well-known example of the value of design, especially design that delivers simplicity, is Apple's iPhone. Steve Jobs possessed an almost religious belief in the power of simplicity. This guiding orientation influenced everything he touched at Apple, which was a lot, considering his CEO status. It shaped how the company was organized, how people got work done, and the products they produced. The arrival of the iPhone in 2007 was a significant milestone not only for Apple but also for consumer design. Prior to this point, people would have separate discrete products to make phone calls, listen to music, and take a photo. The iPhone for the first time integrated the phone, music player, and camera (and later many other functions). The design solution delivered a step change in the balancing of technical, commercial, and human needs. But what was most surprising was how Apple had ingeniously integrated these needs in a product that was so beautifully simple. A single screen with one button. All of the various functions organized in applications. The ability to further organize common applications into groupings. The ease of switching between functions or applications like the music player and the phone. It was pure design brilliance. And consumers responded. It has been a significant driver of Apple's miraculous performance since its inception and has set a high design benchmark for others.

It somehow feels good when complex things are simplified. It could be that you appreciate not having to expend unnecessary energy trying to understand it. It could be that if feels good to save time. It could be that simple things just look pretty. But human beings tend to gravitate toward simple over complex, and companies are starting to finally catch up on this point. Products and experiences are increasingly designed to be as simple as possible. We're seeing companies being successful with one or two products, like Allbirds shoes. They make two types of shoe, both with New Zealand merino wool, and that's it. It's a very simple offering, but the shoes are incredibly comfortable, look good, and consumers love them. CarMax has made the process of buying and selling used cars incredibly simple and easy. They have transformed the traditionally long and painful experience into a couple of simple steps, and it has been a huge hit in the marketplace. People want a product or an experience that is as easy, clear, and as simple as possible. And often consumers are willing to pay a premium for it if it means saving time and/or freeing them of hassles, stress, and frustration.

When I launched my consulting firm in 2014 and was going through the process of establishing all the necessary bits and pieces like a CRM (Salesforce), accounting software (Xero), and a bank account, I decided to go with a bank that I won't name. I remember how painful it was to attempt to get anything done on the bank's online banking site. It was so incredibly convoluted and complicated. Any time I wanted to do online banking, like pay a bill or deposit money, I was incredibly frustrated with how long it would take to do anything and how much energy I would have to expend figuring out the functionality. The site was so busy with content and links and visuals. Just looking at it was dizzying. It took so many steps to do a simple thing, and because there was so much content and so many link options on the one page, trying to find what you were looking for took an age. It felt like the organizational complexity of the big bank was being reflected in their online banking site. It got to the point where I was so frustrated with how complicated the online banking experience was that I decided to close all the business accounts and go with a different bank.

Four a half years later, on a recent trip back to New Zealand, I opened a personal bank account with the Bank of New Zealand, and what a different experience! Logging in to online banking for the first time I was absolutely gobsmacked at how simple the landing page was. They have managed to reduce the page down to the core functions, and it is a thing of beauty. I couldn't believe how much empty space there was on the page. The only visuals were my two accounts, and to transfer money between them all I had to do is drag a specified amount from one account to the other—no drop-down menus with option after option of detail to add. If I want to open another account, all I have to do is click on a + icon. Withdrawing or depositing money takes a couple of seconds. They've just made it so easy, and it feels so good as a customer to be able to achieve what I want in such a simple, time-efficient manner.

When you consider these examples of simplifying product portfolios or customer experiences or how beautifully Apple integrated so much functionality into their simple iPhone product, it's easy to see how there are massive opportunities to simplify work, to simplify organizations and reduce or remove all the low-value, non-core activities that create overhead and prohibit organizational and individual focus. There is so much unnecessary complicated noise within organizations, especially large ones, which results in substantial wasted energy, time, and money. So often I have heard employees within large organizations claim that they can't compete with smaller firms that "don't have as much overhead," which has never made sense to me. Why can't a large organization be as nimble and as efficient as a smaller one? What is the excess overhead that is preventing the company from delivering to customers? Sure, there are basic operational costs that rise with increased size, like office space, systems, and employee salaries, but with size comes the capacity to service more customers, so you would expect the rise in operational costs to be offset by the increased customer base, therefore enabling the same level of agility and pricing as smaller competitors. It seems intuitive that design or "design thinking," if it works on products and consumer experiences, could also help to sort out the debilitating complexity that is holding organizations and individuals back.

How Design Thinking Is Different

Design thinking is an approach that Tim Brown, Tom Kelley, and the team at the design firm IDEO created to illuminate the process they go through in solving problems and creating innovative solutions.[9] Design thinking is quite different from the traditional management consulting approach to problem solving and solutioning, which I learned within big global consulting firms. Design thinking has a number of defining characteristics that set it apart from traditional problem-solving methods. One is taking a human-centered approach versus a purely analytical approach.

Designers see the world through the eyes of the consumer. They put themselves in the shoes of the people who will be using a product or experiencing a service. They take the time to ratchet up their empathy and immerse themselves in the world of the user. It is through this immersion that they reveal

---

9   Tim Brown, *Change by Design* (HarperCollins, 2009).

critical problems to be solved or opportunities to enhance the design of the product or service, whereas a traditional management consulting approach is to be much more data driven. You bring in the Excel jockeys, dump a load of data, and then let them crunch through it and produce a bunch of pretty graphs. The challenge with this latter approach is it often misses the real issues affecting the business or opportunities in the marketplace. The other consideration is that machines will increasingly be able to do the work of data analysis and insight production. Human analytical value will increasingly come from understanding the human experience and seeing and solving those opportunities that can be revealed only through empathy and user immersion.

This human-centered approach is also particularly helpful when pursuing simplification. Truly immersing oneself in the world of the worker reveals all kinds of contextual insights that would never be gathered purely from a survey or from data analysis. Sometimes the opportunities that deliver the greatest impact on crushing complexity are the subtle things that can be identified only through close observation.

I worked with a large financial services company that was experiencing productivity issues and wanted to reveal what could be done to resolve the problem. We rolled out our survey and completed our interviews and identified plenty of good opportunities, like training particular groups on how to manage email and plan and prioritize effectively. But it was one observation that came from simply walking the halls of the organization that provided a very interesting insight that would have macro cultural implications. Everyone seemed to go from one committee to another. The company had created a culture of committees. They would bring people together to talk about everything. Anytime someone produced something—and it could be anything across both front and back offices—there was an implicit requirement to socialize it with as many people as possible. And then as soon as an update was made on the approach, design, or plan, it was resocialized with the same group. This cultural orientation resulted in people spending a significant proportion of their day and week in unnecessary, often low-value meetings. Pieces of work would circle around and around and around. People would think they would get a piece of work to a good place and would then get another piece of feedback that would send it down another track. When this observation was played back to the stakeholder groups, there was a surprised and excited reaction: "You mean that there could be a way of reducing these meetings?" There was clearly some built-up, repressed frustration at the number of these meetings, but the common belief was that they were a necessary part of doing business. This observation led to a substantial effort to evolve the culture away from heavy socialization to one that exemplified more entrepreneurial traits like ownership, fast failing and informal collaboration.

Taking a human-centered approach to problem solving truly reveals how to improve the experience of the person. And in this day and age, with machines taking over so much low-value repeatable work, it makes sense to focus on how to better enable people to do their best work on the most important priorities.

Design thinking is also highly participative. There is a focus on engaging clients and impacted teams throughout the process, from problem solving to solutioning to testing and rollout. There is so much value in getting client individuals and teams involved in the design thinking simplification process. They obviously have all the contextual information and so are the sources of the information required to come up with a solution. They often have a ton of ideas on how to simplify various parts of their role and thus are valuable in the brainstorming and solutioning process. And when they're engaged in the prototyping and iteration process, it fosters buy-in and ownership, which is essential if the solutions are to be embedded into the business and sustained over time.

This approach is quite different from many traditional consulting engagements where the consulting team works quite separately from the client. The consultants are often given a floor to themselves (depending on the size of the project and the client), or they'll be huddled together in a conference room somewhere hidden away. When it comes to the production of the work, junior consultants crunch away by themselves until the work is ready to be reviewed by senior consultants. Once iterations have been made in-house, they're presented back to the client. Given that the client has not participated in the "sausage making," they all nod their heads during the presentation but do not really understand the intricacies of the work or have the desire to bring it to life. This leads to one of the common complaints about consulting firms: "they come in, take up half a floor, produce a bunch of beautiful PowerPoint decks, and then leave." The clients have not been engaged throughout the process and do not have a sense of ownership and co-creation, and therefore when the consultants leave, the work falls flat and the significant investment is wasted.

While engaging client teams in the design thinking simplification process is highly valuable and delivers a bunch of impact, there is one caveat: capacity. You have to be careful with how much time your team soaks up from stakeholder groups. The engagement has to be somewhat targeted. Unless the individuals have been assigned to the effort full time, you should not expect or plan for significantly time-consuming sessions. You have to be conscious that the individuals have a day job, so this should inform how and when they are baked into the process.

Overall, the more engagement from stakeholders in the design thinking simplification process, the better. Their input is essential through the three steps of the design thinking method and is invaluable in the context of pursuing simplification.

The Design Thinking Method for Simplifying Work

The design thinking method can be broken down in a few different ways. The most common sequence of steps in design thinking is:

1. Empathize
2. Define
3. Ideate
4. Prototype
5. Test
6. Implement

Given that we're using the process to drive simplification, six steps seem to be too many. We have found that we can integrate steps 1 and 2, and 4, 5, and 6. The third step, "ideate," warrants its own step. We bake the design thinking core elements into three stages:

1. Empathizing and illuminating
2. Ideation

3. Prototyping and iterative implementation

Here are some descriptions of how these stages come to life.

Step 1: Empathizing and Illuminating

In the empathizing and illuminating phase, our objective is to be able to paint a detailed picture of how an organization influences and enables work. We want to understand what people actually do and how they do it. We capture this information by interviewing stakeholders, facilitating workshops, observing work, and deploying surveys to capture a rich sense of organizational reality for a target group. We ask expansive questions, taking a divergent perspective, to uncover many hidden aspects of the organizational makeup.

During this initial phase of the design thinking simplification approach, there is a strong focus on listening and learning versus telling. Building from the human-centered approach, a priority is clearly placed on building a strong understanding of the targeted context before solutioning can begin. And this can only be achieved through a fierce focus on asking great questions and then shutting up and listening. Many management consultants could take a page out of this book. I have come across many consultants who are much more comfortable walking into an organization and then quickly telling them how they should run their business before learning about the intricacies and unique context of the business. Given this bias to listening, it is important to ask really good questions that help to unlock the reality of current ways of working. The crafting of questions uncovers the intricacies of human interactions and how structure, process, system, and culture influence the experiences of employees and in so doing shines the spotlight on the biggest opportunities.

My father spent his career as a television and print journalist and would often say that getting the story is all about asking the right questions. I remember him saying that "each question has to be delicately crafted, because you run such a fine line between getting the juicy content you need or just pissing off the person, which will quickly shut them up like a clam." I have certainly seen this come to life in my own experiences as a management consultant. Consultants are thrown into a department and need to interview a set of employees who don't know anything about the work the consultants are doing or why they need to speak to an outside person. As a result, they naturally come into the conversation with reservations and skepticism. Asking the wrong questions in these settings can quickly alienate the employees, which essentially halts any progress you hope to make. Taking the time to craft the right questions can quickly put employees at ease and build their confidence in the consultant and the process. Nurturing a sense of co-creation leads to not only gaining the information required but also building support and buy-in for the overall work.

Often you have to ask the same question multiple times in different ways to get to the level of detail that reveals opportunities. My oldest daughter is at the stage where she is asking why about everything. And she'll ask why continually to drill down to as much detail as is possible. It's interesting sometimes trying to respond to the fourth "Why?" Getting to that level of detail is often very revealing as to something's true purpose. Recently I had one of these exchanges with her:

DAUGHTER: Dad, why do you have to travel for your work?

ME: Because I need to work with my clients in person?

DAUGHTER: Why?

ME: Because working in person delivers good results.

DAUGHTER: Why?

ME: Because it's easier to communicate and to collaborate.

DAUGHTER: Why?

ME: Ah…it just is…

Crafting delicate ways of getting to the third or fourth why is a useful questioning objective when pursuing simplification, as it reveals whether something is really necessary.

Another questioning tactic is stripping out consultant speak or corporate talk. Make the questions as easy to understand and relatable as possible. Here is an example of the difference between using consulting speak and simple language in questioning:

- "What is the organizational strategy?" versus "Where will your organization win in the marketplace going forward? Where does your organization make most money? Where is the organization growing the most?"
- "Define your role?" versus "How does your position add value to the organization?"

- "How do you experience complexity?" versus "Which low-value activities take up your time? What distractions and interruptions do you experience?"
- "What opportunities to you perceive to optimize your impact?" versus "Are there tasks or activities that could be removed and reduced to allow you to spend more time on the things that matter most?"

Asking really good questions is not easy, but when done right along with true listening, it reveals insights that accelerate problem solving and innovative solutioning. It is an important focus area as part of the design thinking method.

There are many elements of work to uncover during the empathizing and illuminating phase, influenced, of course, by the scope of work. That said, it is always important to start with the big picture. We always like to start with understanding the organizational strategy and competitive context. Specific questions that can be posed include:

- What value does the company deliver?
- Is the mission clear to people?
- Why do customers choose this company over its competitors?
- What part of the business is growing fastest?
- What is the most profitable part of the business?
- Where will the company need to win in the future?
  - Product / service
  - Geography
  - Customer experience
- What are the critical capabilities that the company needs to possess?

- What external trends are influencing the business?
- What are the risks to the business?
- How would you describe the speed of work today?
- How would describe the quality of innovation today?
- How would you describe employee engagement levels?

In addition to posing these types of questions, it is also helpful to analyze available strategic documentation, including organization charts, enterprise technology plans, strategy plans, and others.

Once a sufficient understanding of the organizational context is established, you can then lean in to the reality of target stakeholder groups. Questions for individuals or teams can include:

- Are you clear on the company's strategy, mission, and values?
- What is the purpose of your role?
- How do contribute to the business's success?
- What are your priorities?
- What non-core activities do you engage in in an average day?
- How much time do you spend on each activity?
- Where do you get the information you need to do your work?
- How many systems do you interact with to do your job?
- How do you collaborate with your team members?
- What are sources of frustration for you in your position?
- How many steps does it take to do [activity]?
- How often do you get interrupted or are distracted?
- What are the sources of the interruptions or distractions?

I would encourage you to linger in the discovery phase for as long as you can. It can be so tempting to jump quickly into solutioning as soon as you've uncovered a couple of opportunities. I'm certainly guilty of quickly pivoting into solutioning, often prematurely, so I need to keep reminding myself to continue to lean into uncovering more context to reveal the complete picture. The more opportunities you can uncover, the better you will be able to reveal and solve the root cause.

Once you have captured sufficient current state information in its many forms, you are ready to start to make sense of it. You can do this by looking for patterns, organizing and visualizing it as much as possible. We develop integrated visual depictions of the company that reveal how structure, system, process, and culture influence and enable (and disable) work. We quantify the amount of work spent on various activities and aggregate sources of frustration. This is where the survey comes in handy. The output of the survey, if the right questions are posed, can easily be converted into graphs that nicely visualize where people are spending their time. This form of analysis is also highly valued with leadership teams. We worked at a large global organization that was struggling with complexity, and the leaders were unsure how to approach it and where to lean in. Being able to sit down and talk through one graph that clearly illustrated the activities that were absorbing people's time enabled decisions to be quickly made on how to redesign roles, responsibilities, processes, and systems to liberate their people from low-value work.

Across the forms of current state analysis, a range of simplification opportunities emerge. These are all captured, grouped, and then prioritized based on their relative impact on performance and ease of implementation. Through the lens of strategy—what is most important for the company to succeed going forward—we determine relative impact on performance. Determining relative ease of implementation is achieved through considering interdependencies, costs, and timeframes. A standard two-by-two matrix that compares impact on performance and ease of implementation can be a helpful and simple way of visualizing which opportunities to pursue.

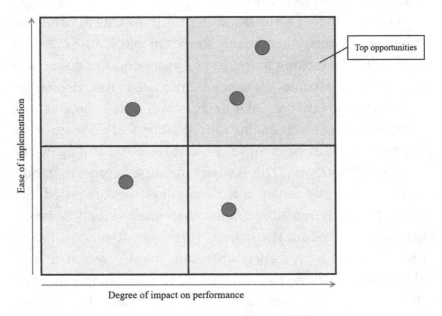

Figure 2.

With the top five opportunities distilled, we can begin the process of ideation.

Step 2: Ideation
The design thinking ideation process promotes bringing together diverse areas of expertise in a small team format to rapidly brainstorm solutions. It is a highly collaborative process

that really encourages innovation and thinking outside the box. There are no bad ideas, so all team members are encouraged to explore any and every avenue to solve the top problems. For effective ideation to occur you need an environment of high trust. People need to feel like the other team members will not judge them on bad ideas. With a foundation of trust there also needs to be a shared "building" mentality. If someone comes up with an interesting idea, others should feel energized to build on the idea, tweak it, evolve it, and/or explore tangents. Without an environment of trust or a building mentality, people simply won't hit for the fences. They will come up with obvious, boring ideas, which will limit breakthrough innovation.

A couple of team design factors influence the degree of trust in a team. They include the size of the team and the strength of the relationships. If the team is too large, say, bigger than six, people begin to go into their shell. The more people in the team, the less likely a single person is to trust the group and open up. Also, if you have a team of people who have never met before, you're also less likely to have a high degree of trust, thus limiting innovative contributions. Ideally, a team no bigger than six with people who have worked with each other or have gone through an effective relationship building exercise is optimal to enable high trust and freeing the creative juices to run rampant on the top opportunities.

Having people in the group from different backgrounds and areas of expertise also fuels highly innovative ideation. At Simplify Work, we bring people together with deep expertise in areas including organization design, culture, Lean Six Sigma, IT, design, and others. Importantly, we also bring in select client individuals into the process to provide additional expertise and deep contextual knowledge. We have found that in going after simplification we are often redesigning organizational elements like strategy, structure, roles, responsibilities, processes, and culture, so having people with deep expertise in these areas is obviously helpful. But at the same time people who have different expertise will chime in with ideas that may not have been considered if the group was made up of people with the same professional background. Thus, having the diversity of thought supports and accelerates the ideation process.

One of the interesting things I have found in working in diverse teams is that it tests my core assumptions or mental models. In one instance when I was working on a diverse team to design a change management center of excellence (CoE), this revelation slapped me in the face. I came into the project after an initial cut had been designed. In my typical way I immediately went after how the design could be simplified to make it more impactful. I began to strip out structures and constraining processes and superfluous responsibilities. An online knowledge repository was being built to provide users with an overview of the change methodology and supporting tools and materials. I immediately translated written content into short video blurbs and reduced the number of tools and examples to the few most meaningful. But at one point during this initiative, a couple of team members were working on defining the purpose of change management and they landed on something like "Change management is critical to our success and intrinsically linked to people's inspiration and development." This definition clashed with my view on change management. To me, change management is essentially how to accelerate the implementation of transformation programs to rapidly realize intended benefits and reduce the risk of failure. It's not linked to people's inspiration or development. It then dawned on me that I had assumed alignment in our team on the core purpose and definition of change management. Without this alignment we would be designing for different objectives, which would clearly lead to downstream design flaws. Now, one of the first steps I encourage when forming an initiative team is aligning on core principles and objectives and not relying on assumptions.

A good ideation process also fuels integrative problem solving, which is essential when dealing with complexity. An integrative thinking approach takes into account multiple tensions while solving the problem versus the traditional analytical approach to problem solving that focuses on one problem at a time. This better enables solving for the many requirements and functions that companies and groups deal with that drive complexity. It also increases the likelihood of designing a solution that targets the root cause versus many low-level spot solutions that don't deliver as much value.

As we have learned there are many drivers of complexity within an organization, including:

- Unclear strategic focus
- Convoluted organizational structure
- Too many layers of management
- Too many low-value, time-consuming meetings
- Multiple approval processes
- Overly prioritized compliance processes

Taking an integrative approach to macro simplification often results in the need for a significant transformation. The transformation would touch many parts of the organization to drive out the various enablers of complexity. As we'll discuss in the next chapter, common target areas include:

- Distilling and communicating a clear, focused strategy
- Streamlining organization design
- Reducing complicated processes, rules, and other clutter
- Simplifying systems
- Redirecting organizational culture

But simplification endeavors can also occur at more focused levels. We work with many organizations that want to simplify a function, group, or team. Or there are specific opportunities at the intersection of specific teams or functions, where complexity is prohibiting effective cross-team or functional collaboration. We also have clients who ask for help in building the right simplified smart habits in their people, which is obviously more of a learning solution than redesigning structure, process, and systems. So, an integrative problem-solving approach can and should be used in tackling complexity at both a macro level as well as at a more targeted level. This orientation simply encourages the consideration of the many drivers of complexity and therefore promotes more innovative solutions that solve many problem areas simultaneously.

Getting to integrative problem solving is influenced by how you diverge and converge during the ideation process. We recommended going very wide with the initial dump of ideas. This is diverging. Any and all ideas on how to solve the problem are encouraged and captured. The wide, diverging nature of this exercise exposes the many elements or tensions that could inform a solution. At a certain point, normally influenced by the project deadline, the team will begin to converge on the ideas. This can take a few different forms, but a common approach is facilitating a working session where sticky notes and little spot stickers play important roles. Each solution idea is captured on a sticky note, and the ideas are then grouped into logical groupings or themes. Everyone is then asked to vote on their top ideas by placing one of their allocated dot stickers to the idea groupings they like the most. The output of this voting reveals the prioritized list of ideas.

It's also helpful to bring back the impact on performance versus ease of implementation matrix as another lens through which to view the solution opportunities.

Once the top three to five solutions have been selected prototyping can begin.

Step 3: Prototyping and Iterative Implementation

Design thinking encourages rapid testing of new solutions. This is done through prototyping and iterative implementation. Prototyping is another unique process when compared with traditional consulting. Normally one solution is proposed and then implementation ensues. With prototyping, the solution ideas coming out of the ideation process are rapidly designed and tested. The intent is to learn as much as you can through experience and then iterate the design based on lessons learned. This can sometimes be tricky when testing a design for a streamlined organization structure or a simplified enterprise technology architecture. But methods such as mapping the employee journey and even role-playing how a different structure, process, or system would affect ways of working are useful. The point is that by rapidly testing a new solution and incorporating the lessons, you improve on the initial solution design and reduce the risk of major failure, which can happen if a solution isn't tested and adjusted prior to implementation.

More often than not traditional consulting teams will pilot a new solution before a full rollout. However, often the scale of the pilots is still pretty large, and only so much change can occur to the original design. Prototyping and rapid testing decrease the scale of the pilot to allow more solutions to be tested and more rounds of feedback to be captured and integrated.

Another method consulting firms use is the hypothesis-driven approach. This means that the consultants arrive, have a couple of conversations, do a bit of analysis, and come up with hypotheses on what the solutions are. It's essentially coming into a problem with solutions already crafted. The idea is that if hypotheses are disproven during deeper analysis, then new hypotheses are created. The challenge is that you get too far along the process with one hypothesis and have invested too much time and effort to radically alter it, even when analysis reveals it may be inaccurate.

A better approach is rapidly testing solution ideas, capturing feedback, incorporating the improvement opportunities, and promoting continual iteration. This last part is important. Even when prototyping has been completed and the new solution is implemented, design thinking encourages ongoing iterations. The learning, adjusting, and evolving of solutions never stops. This promotes a culture of continuous improvement, which stimulates curiosity, ongoing learning, and reflection. Importantly, it also reduces the risk of failure mentality that can stymie innovation at the outset. Many companies have cultures that could be characterized as risk-averse or having a risk of failure. It often manifests in tremendous overanalysis of every piece of work and also leads to oversocialization: "I'll get as many people to review and agree to this plan as possible, so if it fails, it's everyone's fault." We'll talk about this and other cultural traits that drive complexity more in the next chapter. However, prototyping and iterative implementation, if woven into local ways of working, can be a first step to diminishing the risk of failure mentality while optimizing innovative solution design.

Client participation in the prototyping process is highly valuable. Users test the new solutions to see whether they actually achieve the objective of simplifying work to heighten energy and focus on the true top priorities. Due to the involvement of users throughout this process, they naturally become owners of the outcomes, which significantly improves their buy-in of the final solution. From a change management perspective, it is a highly effective technique for reducing resistance and establishing motivated ownership and commitment.

Types of prototype solutions that we have tested in the past include:

- Communications to synthesize and clarify an organizational strategy
- Streamlined work processes
- New system interface
- Small team structures
- Mechanisms to reinforce new behaviors

The nature of the prototype will obviously influence which testing option is used. As mentioned earlier, useful ways of prototyping things that affect an experience include role modeling and/or testing an idea or solution on a sample population. However, when role modeling, you clearly need to have some good actors on staff.

Given that the idea is to test the solution ideas in a rapid way, the prototypes certainly do not need to be perfect. The intent is to capture feedback on the core design elements, like the removal of certain approval processes or a new way to measure and manage performance reviews. Feedback is captured and aggregated, and key themes are revealed. Updates are made, and then the new version is tested again. Once we have completed a prototyping process and have integrated lessons learned, we are ready to roll out the solution(s).

One significant determinant of implementation success and sustainability is leadership commitment. The reality is that without staunch leadership commitment, the simplification solutions will fall flat. There has to be a commitment to the simplification agenda, which means that there has to be a belief in the value of what simplification can deliver for a business. It is so easy for things to fall back the way they were without leaders continuing to model and enforce new ways of working. I recently worked with a large global consumer packaged goods client that was really struggling with complexity. The company had gone through a dramatic global operating model transformation to strip out cost across the business. They installed global shared service centers, underwent significant reductions in force, centralized a traditionally decentralized global structure, and installed zero-based budgeting. In an industry where growth is very sluggish, this would seem to be the right strategic move to bolster margins. The business experienced a challenge when they removed all the support resources while launching the shared service centers. They found that it wasn't a one to one transfer of activities. Thus, highly paid experts in functions such as marketing, sales, and strategy all of a sudden had a lot more administrative burden, which immediately pulled them from higher-value work. More and more noise started to emanate from these functions. People were clearly unhappy with the increased distractions and their inability to keep on top of everything. Quality started to suffer. The company was traditionally recognized as an innovator and leader in marketing excellence. This reputation started to be impacted as subpar campaigns littered the media. Then key people started to leave. When leadership received the output of their annual global engagement survey, they knew they had to act. The global marketing and sales functions had the worst engagement scores in the company and were well below the industry average. An engagement agenda was created, and part of it targeted the complexity challenge. Levers that were pulled to drive simplification included adding additional administrative support, removing or simplifying clunky systems, lifting reporting requirements, and pushing decision-making authority down into the businesses. These were great levers to go after and clearly high pain points for the affected groups. We managed to coordinate the regional teams and get alignment on simplification plans, but unfortunately we couldn't quite get the leadership ownership we needed. While they certainly recognized the need and agreed with the strategy, they didn't feel they had the time to actively model or reinforce the new ways of working. As a result, progress was slow and the value of simplification remained untapped.

However, something interesting happened during a dramatic global cyberattack that caused all critical systems across the company's global operations to crash and stay off. For a two-week period, all email was down and no one could access their online calendar, so they weren't able to attend meetings. When the systems came back online, I was fortunate to attend a couple of review meetings. I was expecting to hear a lot of frustration and concern about how behind everyone felt, but instead it was the opposite. People felt absolutely liberated during the systems crash. All of a sudden people were freed from all obligations: peripheral projects, compliance requirements, committees, and many other time sucks. There were no piles of emails to work through. So, what did everyone do? They focused their time on their top priorities – marketing leaders met personally with key stakeholders like market sales leads to work on critical campaigns. Salespeople met key leads in person and strengthened relationships and/or closed deals. They felt for the first time like they were able to truly focus on their top priorities. Many said that the two-week period was the most productive of the year. Leaders' eyes were all of sudden opened to the value of simplification and the debilitating effect complexity can have on performance. This experience was the catalyst the simplification work needed to gain true leadership support. The impact that the leadership commitment and ownership had on the simplification program has been significant, and now the global organization is well on its way to establishing key simplification drivers, including empowering people across the business to stamp out unnecessary complexity where they see it.

Another key determinant of implementation success is change management. As noted earlier, having the users participate in the process is one effective means of fostering buy-in, but more will need to be done to embed change, especially if the solutions are transformational in nature.

Traditionally, change management was overly focused on a highly formulaic process with specific steps that should be adhered to like an audit trail. Each consulting firm would tout their "methodology" as unique, but really they are all largely the same. Each method includes doing an upfront assessment on objectives, stakeholders, and the types of impacts. This information informs the design of a change strategy and the more detailed communications and training plans. In some methods they include change agent strategies and feedback mechanisms. But the real magic of change management is in the design and delivery of the tactics that actually affect a groups' understanding of and buy-in to a set of changes. This magic often comes from deep expertise in behavioral economics and neuroscience.

We often think that we are highly rational and logical and make decisions based on facts and figures, but in reality we are emotional beings who are influenced by many social and psychological factors. Behavioral economics, based on psychological analysis, has identified a range of human biases in how we make decisions. These biases or emotional triggers can be manipulated to drive acceptance and buy-in during the roll-out of organizational changes. They include:

- **Framing effect:** How something is introduced influences perception.
- **Nudges:** Indirect suggestions influence decision making.
- **Loss aversion:** Loss is more painful than a gain is pleasurable.
- **Status quo basis:** People have a preference for the current state of affairs.
- **Anchoring:** We rely heavily on the first piece of information given.

- **Herd behavior:** People follow the group.
- **Reciprocity:** If you give something to someone, they feel obliged to do something in return.
- **Choice overload:** Having too many choices limits decision making.

Each tactic can be used in different ways to influence behavior in many diverse arenas and certainly during change campaigns.

The framing effect is used extensively in communicating change. Key messages are crafted to alter people's perception of a change. For example, instead of saying "we are implementing a new system that will require you to spend a week to learn how to use it," you could say "we are implementing a new system that will help you spend more time on your highest-priority activities."

Herd behavior is another tactic this is often used: creating an impression that everyone else is doing something. People naturally want to follow the group. Maybe this tactic should be called the sheep tactic. A message that uses this tactic could be: "Don't be left behind; join the hundreds of people benefiting from this product."

Choice overload is an important simplification concept. Having too many choices paralyzes decision making. When introducing changes, it is important to limit the options to ideally two or three. This not only accelerates decision making but also limits the risk of cognitive overload. There are many important applications of this tactic beyond effective change management, such as how you design a product or a customer experience.

Intelligent change management weaves the behavioral economic levers together in carefully crafted communications and engagement tactics that facilitate the introduction of new changes, get people to learn and feel comfortable, and then embed new ways of working as part of the process.

Neuroscience provides a psychological tangent to behavioral economics. Neuroscience research reveals how our brains work. It illuminates how different parts of our brain are responsible for different cognitive functions. The prefrontal cortex is an area in the front of our brain where we do all our executive functioning, like strategic planning and problem solving. Other, more primal parts of the brain are responsible for functions like hunger, sexual attraction, and the fight-or-flight response. The latter of these is managed in an area of the brain called the amygdala. The amygdala is triggered anytime someone feels threatened, and once it is triggered it becomes very difficult to think clearly, retain information, and innovate. If you want people to be doing their best work, you don't want them to be in a state of threat. You also don't want people to feel threatened during change as it significantly slows the adoption process. David Rock put together a framework to help us understand the specific threat triggers so that we can sculpt communications and change events to help prevent these debilitating cognitive occurrences. The framework is called SCARF,[10] and these are the triggers:

- **Status:** when status is threatened or diminished
- **Certainty:** not knowing what will happen next

---

10   David Rock, *Your Brain at Work* (HarperCollins, 2009), 195–197.

- **Autonomy factor:** ability to make decisions for yourself
- **Relatedness:** when people feel cut off from social interactions
- **Fairness:** perception that an event or situation is unfair

To bring the SCARF triggers to life in a change context a set of carefully crafted tactics would generate excitement about the program by outlining the benefits to the business and the individuals. The messages would be delivered by someone who is respected and trusted. Everyday language would be used to increase the sense of authenticity, which is especially important for Generation X and Millennials.

Communications would also clearly lay out the timeline of events so that people know what's coming up and what is expected of them. Rich interactions between impacted stakeholders and their managers would be organized to reduce concerns about status and to consolidate excitement about the benefits of the program. Participation in problem solving and solution design would be encouraged to create a sense of ownership. Community events would be scheduled to discuss and capture feedback on and solutions for improvement opportunities.

Infusing behavioral economics and neuroscience into the design of change management tactics is what really generates the sustainable accelerated adoption of new ways of working. Clearly, the right change management plays a key role in making simplification solutions stick.

The third step in the design thinking approach to simplification is clearly an important one. As those that have experienced transformation programs will attest, the most challenging part of the process is the execution. Prototyping and iterative implementation are helpful mechanisms to not only optimize solutions but also pursue ongoing improvements beyond implementation. With high user engagement, strong leadership commitment, and creative change management, the successful execution of solutions will unleash the performance potential of simplifying work.

The design thinking method is an effective way of structuring how to simplify work. The process fosters highly innovative ways of simplifying work across a business. Based on our experience in simplifying organizations, we see some common areas that are targets for simplification. Let's now explore some of these typical areas that deliver the greatest impact on crushing complexity and liberating innovation, productivity, and engagement.

CHAPTER 3

Common Simplification
Focal Areas

M any parts of a business can create confusion, cloud focus, and absorb time and energy. But some specific areas generate the lion's share of this muddy state. Here are some of the common tactics that target these key sources of complexity.

Simplifying Strategy

As organizations grow they often expand into new business units and geographies. They identify new opportunities to diversify a product, go into a peripheral business, and/or enter new markets. They also can acquire other companies to add capability, broaden a product portfolio, or become more vertically integrated. All of this expansion has traditionally resulted in a lot more complexity. More structures, processes, rules, and responsibilities are defined to maintain control of the expanding workforce, and strategic focus gets hazy. It places more burden on the back-office function, increases the number of "strategic initiatives," and adds more layers that separate leadership from the front line.

Many large organizations become bogged down in this complexity, and their performance starts to suffer. Focus is broken, and businesses often lose their edge. The quality of their innovation becomes poor, decision making slows, and execution is error-ridden. Smaller or more agile competitors begin to capture market share with their new innovative products and responsive services. This slide can happen quickly. Consumers are very quick to provide product or service reviews on the plethora of rating sites, and negative reviews can quickly turn from whispers to full-blown movements. This is often when a new CEO is brought in to drive a turnaround. Interestingly, there is one common tactic that leaders deploy to successfully turn around a business: they shed all extraneous business units and return clarity and focus to the business. They simplify strategy.

Steve Jobs famously did exactly this at Apple. When he rejoined Apple in 1997, the first thing he did was complete a review of Apple's product portfolio. At the time, Apple had over 20 distinct products, including my namesake: the Apple Newton. The company was clearly pulled too thin. Leadership had felt that Apple should be present in all industry segments that their competitors were in, so it continued to expand the product portfolio to establish this comprehensive presence.

However, Apple's unique value proposition became unclear to both employees and customers. The performance of the company reflected this in its continued slide, which by 1997 had become serious. Jobs felt the company was months away from bankruptcy. In his mind he was crystal clear on where Apple would win: he did not want a product presence in every category; instead he wanted to build a few of the best products in the world. He moved quickly to sell off underperforming business units and reduced the number of products from 20 to four. He removed legacy leadership and anyone else he felt was not pulling their weight and carefully selected new talent in key roles who were empowered to act and innovate as they saw fit. He removed 11 years' worth of complex and complicated processes and management hierarchy. He stripped out committees and cumbersome approval processes and freed teams to truly innovate on the top strategic priorities. The new simplified strategy was clear, and Jobs was uncompromising in bringing it to life through transforming structure, process, roles, responsibilities, and culture. Apple was now in the business of building a small set of products that would change the world. And now everyone knew it and could work in unison to realize it. Needless to say, the simplification of Apple produced incredible results, which is reflected in Apple currently being the most valuable company in the world.

The success of Apple's turnaround is evidence that large organizations that are failing to perform often have to shrink to rediscover their mojo. They have to shed non-core businesses, streamline or remove clunky processes, reduce corporate costs, and remove redundant controls and checks.

Another example is Lego. Lego experienced a great run of success from its founding in 1932 up until the 1990s. This success was due to keeping the company focused on its core business: producing interlocking plastic bricks. But in the 1990s the company began to rapidly expand into peripheral businesses, such as television programs, video games, theme parks, retail stores, and others. All of these businesses pulled resources and clouded strategic focus. None of them were successful and led to Lego experiencing a decade of decline. Then enter a new CEO in 2004: Jørgen Vig Knudstorp. Like Jobs, Knudstorp completed his organizational review and then quickly set about returning focus to the organization. He knew that he needed to return the company to its core to enable profitable and sustainable growth. He shrunk the portfolio of assets, including selling part of the Legoland theme park, and either closed down or halted expansion plans across the confusing array of business units—dolls, magazines, computer games, television shows, software, and so on. But Knudstorp didn't stop there; he even simplified the Lego core offering by reducing the number of colors and components used. The newfound simplification of the business and the return to the core business liberated focus and innovation. Teams were now able to rejuvenate and refresh their key product: interlocking bricks. A number of innovations sparked renewed market interest in their product, including giving customers the ability to design their own Lego set and increasing co-branded products like the *Frozen* and *Star Wars* lines. Since the simplification of Lego's strategy, the company has achieved a 400% increase in revenues and has boosted the profit margin from –21% to +34%—an incredible turnaround due in large part to simplifying strategy.

There are many other examples of organizations that have simplified their strategy to turnaround their business. IBM sold off their PC business as part of their turnaround. McDonald's has shrunk significantly since their new CEO, Steve Easterbrook, took over in 2015, and positive results are returning. Clearly, reducing strategic distractions and becoming clearer on the focus of the company is an effective method of breathing life back into ailing businesses.

Sometimes organizations simply need to pare down the number of initiatives they have running at one time to regain strategic clarity. Running too many initiatives often occurs when an organization has too many strategic priorities or does not have an adequate initiative review and approval process. Having too many strategic priorities and initiatives running at one time pulls resources too thin, creates competing demands on people's time, and essentially reduces focus. Instead of doing a few things really well, organizations often focus on doing many things adequately or poorly. This particular driver of complexity is one of the most common in my experience. In one simplification project we worked on the organization did a tally of all the strategic initiatives it had running at the one time. The total came to 42. This was eye-opening for the client. They knew they had a lot of initiatives running at one time but didn't realize the extent. It was no wonder debilitating complexity had taken hold in their organization and they were experiencing major performance issues. Thus, one of the first things they did was distill their strategic focus so that they could begin culling initiatives. This organization had gone through sweeping cost-cutting programs over the prior years and was now focused on growth. They used this focus on growth as the lens to review all initiatives in play. They eventually were able to reduce this list from 42 to 12, and it wasn't easy. People who had invested significant time and effort into their initiative obviously were quite resistant to having their project suspended. Each team felt that their initiative was of high strategic importance, which is natural, but means that leadership had to be tough and committed to the cause. Fast-forward a year and the organization was doing a lot less but doing things well. Their R&D function was producing higher-quality innovation, their marketing teams were winning more awards, people were clearly more focused, and this all translated into an uptick in sales.

Another method for simplifying strategy is to simply ensure that everyone knows what the strategy actually is. It is surprising how often employees are not truly clear on what is most important in their business. The essence of strategy may be clear to a few individuals at the top of the organization, but it may not be clear to the rest. There is where an effective communication campaign can play an important part in building collective understanding and buy-in for an organization's strategy.

It's funny; when you ask, "What is truly most important for the company?" people's natural reaction is to think, "Well, that's obvious," but when they actually start to attempt to verbalize what it is, they quickly get stumped. Most people are so busy in their day-to-day job that they don't stop to think about what the broader company is trying to achieve and how that affects them. They obviously know how the company makes money (usually), but in terms of what capabilities the company needs to build or the markets and customer segments that they need to target, most are usually a little hazy. This lack of strategic clarity is often overlooked but is an important enabler of complexity. Without a clear understanding of an organization's strategic priorities, one cannot make decisions on priorities and therefore is less able to say no to things. Establishing alignment on the few things that the company needs to do to win gives employees the target to work toward. It naturally brings focus for many disparate teams and gets people all running in the same direction. It also makes it easier to identify those things that are getting in the way.

But effectively communicating a strategy can be quite challenging. It is hard to communicate a strategy that people can quickly understand, get excited about, and remember. Often the communication of strategies, if it happens at all, is far too detailed, boring, and simply not engaging. As a result, the strategy falls on deaf ears and people go back to going through the motions in their roles.

There are many aspects to the art of effectively communicating a strategy. All the complex elements of a strategy need to be distilled into a pithy, succinct statement or a visual. Language is crucial, so each word needs to be carefully selected. The simpler the language, the better. Consultant-speak or corporate jargon is great for making insecure types sound important and smart but essentially serves to fog meaning. An example would be:

Consultant-speak strategy statement: We will optimize shareholder value via the delivery of products and services that exceed customer expectations.

Common language strategy statement: We will produce the best [product/service] in the world.

When complex strategic aspirations are distilled into a few key messages it can also create a shared language in the organization. The key messages are repeated and reinforced during random meetings and conversations and become part of the language. Changing the nomenclature or shared language in an organization can be a powerful catalyst for aligning focus and changing behaviors to shift culture in line with the strategy.

When communicating anything of importance, the focus must be on clarity. Throughout the process of crafting communications, especially when communicating a strategy or vision, you have to keep asking yourself, "How can I make this clearer? How can I speed understanding? How can this be more memorable? What is most important?"

An example of this is a piece of work I did with the global finance function of a large consumer packaged goods client. The function was in the midst of a transformation where they were seeking to reduce costs by installing regional shared service centers and streamlining processes. The CFO had been in the role for only a year and wanted to convey his vision for the function. A global town hall was scheduled, and we then had to create an effective way of communicating his vision. He provided some high-level guidance on what he wanted his vision to entail, but it was up to us to create the visuals and key messages that would form the core of the global event. The function was a highly complex global structure with many different subgroups operating in different geographies and behaving in different ways. So, with our adult learning hats on, we begin sketching different visual options that brought together the vision, new operating model, and desired culture. As we refined the visual we continued to remove all unnecessary non-core content and eventually landed on a clean, clear, and engaging visual that captured the complexity of the function. The image integrated critical capabilities, operating model priorities, and three core behaviors to lead desired ways of working. It was anchored with the synthesized vision: Global finance: contemporary and world class. The CFO delivered a highly engaging global town hall, and his global team was able to quickly understand the vision, their core capabilities, and how the vision will be realized through the new structure and operating model. Leaders shared stories of how they have seen the critical behaviors come to life, which helped everyone understand the importance of the ways of working and how they can be embodied during day-to-day work. Later that year a global engagement survey revealed that the global finance function engagement score rose by 7%, which was an incredible result and a testament to the positive impact that a clear and engaging vision can have on a population.

How the communication is delivered is also critical. The messages need to be displayed or delivered in a way so that it is rapidly understandable, energizing, and easily retainable. This is often done by carefully visualizing complex content, using metaphors, and storytelling. As much as possible, words should be converted to visuals. As the saying goes, "A picture is worth a thousand words," so using visuals can significantly accelerate understanding of complex points. Also, there are more subtle parts of a visual that can influence a response. The colors within the visual, the amount of white space, and the use of human emotion all affect how someone perceives something. Think of Apple's ads: they master the power of white space. Their message is simple and potent. They make it easy to quickly understand and remember the point they're making: remember "Think different"? You could think of this as mass cognitive manipulation, which it somewhat is. Your goal as a communication expert is to get people to rapidly understand the strategy, get excited by it, and remember it. You're essentially an ad man targeting a bunch of workers.

Metaphors also help to accelerate understanding of a potentially complex topic. Our brain paints a picture of the analogy, which speeds understanding of the material. *Like a thoroughbred bolting ahead of the pack at the Kentucky Derby, we need to be faster and better than our competitors.* These metaphors, when used in a story format, optimize message retention. We remember content a lot easier when delivered in story format because humans have been sharing knowledge for eons through the format of storytelling. Think about people sitting around a fire a thousand years ago sharing tales of their ancestors. We get pulled into stories, especially those involving emotion or human challenges. It's easier to retain concentration and follow along when content is being communicated via a story. If you think back to a recent presentation you have attended, you probably remember a story, not the other content. While many leaders think that a quick email or a one-way video conference will do the trick to align the organization on strategy, there is actually a lot of craft that goes into communicating a strategy so that it sticks. And the effort to communicate a strategy properly is worth the time and energy, because without collective alignment, complexity is much more likely to creep in and people will lose sight of what is truly important.

Crushing complexity and simplifying work often starts at the top, with strategy. It is hard to sustainably simplify work if an organization retains a convoluted strategy. As many large organizations have discovered, stripping away distracting parts of a business can re-energize it through liberating clarity and focus. The performance power of getting the many to focus on the few is incredible. Simplifying strategy and clearly communicating it is often the catalyst for simplifying other parts of an organization, including structure, process, systems, and culture.

Rethinking Organization Design

How a company is structured is often a significant driver of complexity. An organization's structural design directly affects how people get work done, how goals are set, how decisions are made, how communications flow, and how the degree of control influences accountability and autonomy. The traditional 20th-century organization structure has a few, probably recognizable, characteristics:

- Decisions are made at the top of the organization.
- To enable top-line decision making, leaders constantly require status reports and data.
- Leaders control performance by establishing strict processes, policies, role definitions, and performance expectations.
- Middle managers are installed with budgets to manage the execution of the front line.
- Front-line employees follow instructions, adhering to established processes and rules.
- Information is shared on a need-to-know basis.
- Engagement with other groups needs to funnel through management

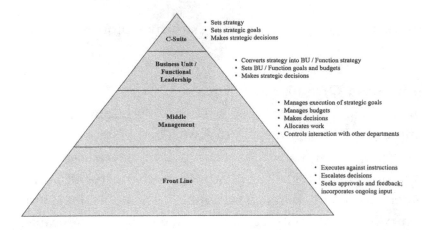

Figure 3.

It is a highly analytical approach to designing an organization. The hierarchical model treats an organization like a machine in which human beings are cogs that produce a predictable outcome. Thus employees should be controlled so that mistakes are limited and productivity baselined. Ongoing improvements can be made by redesigning their processes, but these improvements are obviously made at the top of the organization. The assumption is that the employees at the bottom should simply execute and not get distracted by thinking about better ways of doing something. The belief was that those at the bottom also do not have the intellectual horsepower to come up with meaningful ideas anyway.

The 20th-century approach to organization design led to a number of harmful implications.

- It breeds a reactionary, instruction-following workforce.
- Thinking is discouraged, as the focus is on following predetermined processes and adhering to rules.

- Decision making is slow due to multiple approval processes.
- Innovation is low, as multiple rejections crush willingness to even try.
- There is a heightened sense of anxiety due to "success" being determined by the performance review of a manager.
- Focus shifts to getting through the day and week, not on delivering an output.
- The distance between leadership and the frontline is large; coupled with high-level reporting, this results in suboptimal decision making and missed customer opportunities.
- It breeds a highly political environment, as everyone is vying for more power.
- It creates manager roles that do not add any value.

I'm sure everyone who has worked in an organization has their own stories for how these characteristics have come to life for them. I remember one instance where the last two bullet points came to life for me. I was leading the change management workstream of a large project at an alcoholic beverages company when a new internal director of change management role was filled. The new person set about immediately clarifying that she was my boss and established weekly reports. She also took the seat at the table in steering group meetings. It quickly became apparent that she wasn't going to do any actual work; she just craved the power and status of the role. She loved having people reporting to her and being able to provide what she thought was value-adding direction. She would then report on all the progress I had made during the leadership team meetings.

Needless to say, when the project ended and I moved on to another client, she didn't last long in the role.

One of the challenges with the traditional approach to organizational design is that there is no focus on simplification. In the organization structure design projects I did while a consultant at the big consulting firms, we never considered how to design in a simplified fashion. We followed the typical process of completing a current state assessment, followed by designing high-level structure options, which normally were the typical centralized, decentralized, or matrix structures. We then facilitated workshops to select the preferred model. Once the high-level model was selected, we built out the detail, including management layers, spans of control, reporting relationships, role definitions, capability requirements, RACI charts, decision rights, and performance metrics. The more detail, the better. And the more management control of their teams, the better. This often led to granular process definition, including all the approval subprocesses, reporting cadence, and key performance metrics. When rolling out the new structure, employees only had to adhere to their defined role description and associated processes to do a "good job." To be fair, this was the appropriate approach for the time. Technological capabilities like machine learning and automation did not exist at this time, so many people were still in roles where their responsibility was to manage a repeatable, transactional process. Building out the finer detail as part of a new organization structure was necessary.

The most common organization structure type that most large businesses have today is a matrix. This structure is the most common because it caters to complex organizations that have multiple business units operating in markets around the world. Back-office functions are commonly integrated into regional shared service centers to achieve economies of scale and service all front-office functions. The business units are either organized by market, product, or service. This structure often looks something like Figure 4.

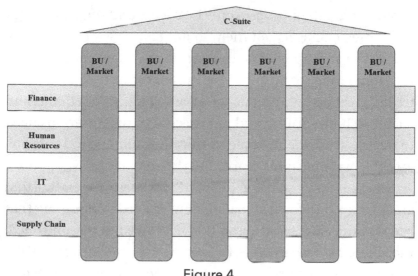

Figure 4.

The challenge with matrix organizations is that people get lost in the web of functions, product groups, customer segments, and geographies. They become territorial with their resources and talent, not willing to share them with other parts of the business that may need them. People also become unclear on the organization's broader strategy and mission and gravitate to their little silo. Coordination across groups becomes a nightmare, so managers add more reporting requirements, more templates to fill in, and more approvals to ensure oversight of performance. And as organizations' performance start to wane due to their internal complexity mess they most often respond by adding more structure and process. As Warren

Bennis said: "Troubled organizations tend to be over-managed and under-led."[11]

However, rapid changes to the business landscape fueled by accelerating technology developments are demanding that organizations innovate well and fast. No longer can companies afford to have their people come into work and simply do what their three managers tell them to do. Employees can't blindly follow the strict predefined processes and then meet with at least four groups of people to get the approvals needed to begin testing preconceived product or service designs. To facilitate and enable rich innovation and fast execution, organizations need to start to trust their people so that they are free to innovate, execute, make mistakes, learn, and thrive.

Companies are starting to explore new ways of operating that are counter to the traditional models. Instead of assuming that people cannot be trusted and therefore need to be controlled, the emerging designs serve to liberate the intelligence of their people by empowering them with the autonomy to work, decide, and execute as they see fit. Progressive organization structures strip out bureaucracy, connect leaders with the front line, and push decision making down to where the information is. While every industry is different and every organization has its unique context, there are likely many opportunities for any organization to simplify how they organize work to better foster innovation, productivity, and engagement.

This autonomous team structure, otherwise referred to as an agile organization or holacracy, is getting more and more attention. An increasing number of organizations, both small and large, are taking steps to move to this progressive structural

---

11 Warren Bennis, *Leaders: Strategies for Taking Charge* (Collins Business Essentials, 2007).

design. The major differences from the traditional model that this relatively new organization structure embodies include:

- **Clarity from the top:** Vision, mission and strategy are set and clearly articulated by leadership. Key opportunities are distilled and translated into a prioritized set of initiatives that are allocated to the appropriate team(s) to pursue.
- **Removal of layers of management:** Vertical reporting lines are removed and replaced with pods of small teams. Layers of management are stripped out, which better connects leadership with the front line and generally improves communication flows.
- **Category pods:** Pods are established for each particular product, service, or market. Within each pod are a number of small teams that work on a particular opportunity.
- **Small autonomous teams that are focused on a particular opportunity:** Each team determines how they solve problems and make decisions, when to execute, and how to incorporate lessons learned.
- **Coordinating nodes:** Teams are closely coordinated through ongoing formal and informal check-ins of various sorts with coordinating groups or nodes.
- **Managers become coaches:** Traditional managers are redeployed as coaches, and their role is to enable effective teaming, mitigate conflict, and provide feedback and coaching.

Visually, this more progressive and simplified structure can look like Figure 5.

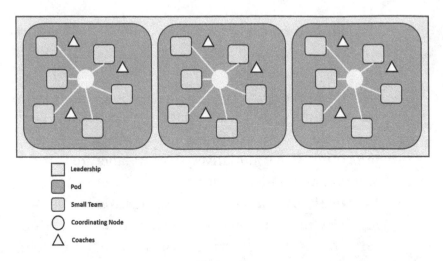

Leadership
Pod
Small Team
Coordinating Node
Coaches

Figure 5.

There are many different ways of bringing the core principles of an agile organization to life for a particular company. There can be models where front-office functions are transformed into agile teams and back-office functions retain their legacy structure but adopt agile ways of working. There are different ways of creating team structures, including the number of people, areas of expertise to include, the broader pod or squad structure, and the governance structure. The agile organization or holacracy structure should not be blindly rolled out without careful consideration of a company's strategic context. It should be adjusted to the specific needs of each company. But there is certainly opportunity for any company operating in a legacy model to infuse elements of the agile blueprint into their operating model, such as breaking down bureaucracy, focusing and clarifying the mission, and empowering the workforce. The results of the transformation can be tremendous and revive companies that have long struggled to achieve the performance they desire.

Based on our experience, a few critical elements of the new organizational model serve to liberate innovation and productivity while ensuring ongoing tight strategic alignment and operational efficiency:

- **Strategic clarity:** Organizational strategy is distilled into one to three strategic priorities. This focus ensures that all initiatives and opportunities stay in line with it, reducing the risk of initiative overflow.
- **Strong and clear values from the top:** Leaders set the clear operating parameters by establishing and enforcing a strong mission and values. These provide the guiding light for how employees should behave, collaborate, execute, and learn in the simplified and open structure.
- **Information transparency:** There should be a constant stream of strategic insights, including customer trends, competitive moves, and new technology developments, that can be readily accessed by anyone in the organization. This enables ongoing prioritization and strategic decision making and fuels innovation.
- **Careful recruitment and training:** Not all people thrive in a small autonomous team environment. Some prefer defined roles and responsibilities and processes they can follow. Thus, recruiting the right people becomes essential. The ability and desire to team effectively must be increasingly emphasized in the recruiting process. Also, training programs should be designed and in place to further strengthen how to effectively build relationships, collaborate, and innovate in team settings.

- **Performance management that recognizes team output:** People should be recognized based on their team's output, thereby incentivizing effective teaming versus the traditional focus on purely individual contributions.

- **Redesigned career path:** Junior employees, especially Millennials, desire lots of feedback and want to know that they are progressing in their career, so a clear career path plays an important role. In the small autonomous team structure, team members progress in their level of seniority based on their contributions to the team. Their development is accelerated through the autonomy they have to try new things, innovate, and learn from mistakes. There is also a lot of cross-pollination across team members and additional development support from the floating coaches.

Human beings do not thrive in controlling environments. With a clear mission and values, humans should be trusted to think, create, and execute. Leaders who take this approach will find that performance is stronger in these organizational conditions versus the traditional controlling approach.

A good analogy for this modern structure is found in societal structure. Compare the productive output of countries that have freedom versus those that don't. What breakthrough innovations came out of the Soviet Union during the USSR era? Lada automobiles? Don't get me started on my Lada jokes. Compare the output of the USSR with countries like Sweden, Germany, the United States, and New Zealand, where people are free to live, discover, and create as they see fit. Life-enhancing inventions emerge like Skype, the iPhone, and merino wool shoes. In a controlling environment, a ceiling is created on what can be produced. Thinking, innovation, and discovery are prohibited, so creative potential is squandered. With a clear set of rules or laws in place and a clear vision, free people can do amazing things.

Supercell, a Helsinki-based games developer, attributes the company's success to their progressive small team or cell structure. Instead of installing a typical bureaucratic structure with layers of managers controlling what employees do, Supercell provides its people complete freedom and responsibility. They prioritize entrepreneurship, autonomy, and speed. They bring this to life through the careful recruitment of individuals who are independent, passionate, and proactive. They then bring these individual contributors together in small teams to work independently on the highest-priority opportunities. Each team has the freedom to make decisions and execute as they wish. Supercell's most successful game, Clash of the Titans, was developed and rolled out by a team of five. As founder and CEO Ilkka Paananen says, "We wanted to ignite the creativity in our people."[12]

Zappos is another example of a company that flattened their organization structure to redistribute authority across the organization. They moved to a small, autonomous team-based structure because their leaders felt that bureaucracy decreased productivity and innovation. As Jon Wolke from the Zappos Insights team says, "Small innovations and changes come more easily now, since the need for approval to try something new is gone."[13] However, it wasn't all roses and sunshine for

---

12 "How Can Company Culture and Structure Empower Employees to Innovate?" EY, https://betterworkingworld.ey.com/workforce/how-can-company-culture-and-structure-empower-employees-to-innovate, accessed October 21, 2017.
13 "How Can Company Culture and Structure Empower Employees to Innovate?" EY, https://betterworkingworld.ey.com/workforce/how-can-company-culture-

Zappos. They found that they went a little too far with freeing their people and experienced a lack of strategic alignment and duplication of work. There is clearly a lot of value in evolving an organization model to empower people, but each company needs to carefully create a model that will work in their unique commercial environment.

Moving to an agile organization can be quite an undertaking, especially if the shift is from the traditional organizational model. The transformation will have many implications beyond structure, including culture, recruitment, reskilling, and strategy.

ING, the Netherlands-based financial services organization, went through a significant organization-wide transformation to become agile in 2015. The company wanted to introduce a new model that would enable the company to rapidly flex and adjust to new customer opportunities. They wanted to minimize handover and bureaucracy and empower people. They brought cross-functional people together in small teams called squads to create new innovative solutions for their customers inspired by a common definition of success. The squads include a "product owner," who operates like a project manager, and a "chapter lead," who provides HR services, such as knowledge sharing across squads, and individual development and coaching. The squads belong to a tribe that is organized by product or service category, which includes a tribal leader. Tribes align each squad through portfolio planning, scrums, and daily stand-ups with the product owners. ING's transformation to agile was comprehensive and included reviewing all legacy employees, making each person reapply for open roles and redesigning the physical layout of their offices to promote informal connectivity, thereby reducing the need for formal meetings. Radically morphing their structure to promote autonomy, empowerment, and collaboration has delivered many performance enhancements such as being quicker to market, improved employee engagement scores, and improved customer experience. ING continues to look ahead to see how they can further evolve their agile model.

One quote that really captures the opportunity that lies within agile is from Magnus Kilian from Qamcom, a Swedish telecommunication company: "The growth and the ideas are not limited to the ideas of management—it's the total knowledge and the total intelligence in the company that we want to get out."[14]

Organization designers' top priority needs to be enabling and encouraging the best thinking from their people. Technology will increasingly take over all repeatable and rules-based work, so the time is right to simplify organizations, strip out bureaucracy, and set the intelligence of people free.

Stripping Out Bureaucratic Practices

What is bureaucracy? Bureaucracy is often thought of as incomprehensible rules and time-wasting procedures. But there are many ways it can come to life in an organization. Think overly cumbersome compliance and controls. What about the multiple rounds of approvals a piece of work may need? Then there is the manager you need to go through to talk to someone in another department. Essentially, all of these things are

---

14   "How Can Company Culture and Structure Empower Employees to Innovate?" EY, https://betterworkingworld.ey.com/workforce/how-can-company-culture-and-structure-empower-employees-to-innovate, accessed October 21, 2017.

getting in the way of productivity and innovation, and serve to disengage people.

Governments are well known for being hotbeds for bureaucratic practices. I was absolutely shocked at how bureaucracy came to life when I recently attempted to renew my daughter's passport at a Chicago post office. First, you can't renew a child's passport online; you have to find one of the few locations that process passport applications and then physically go there to submit the documentation. Then, given that I was renewing my daughter's passport, there is more sensitivity around it; both parents need to be physically present for the submission. Because my wife couldn't be there, she had to get another form filled in and notarized. I arrived at the post office during the week with all the forms and then was told that my daughter had to also be physically present. The thing is that this post office processes passport applications only between 10 a.m. and 3 p.m., Monday through Saturday. My daughter goes to school during the week, so we had to return on a Saturday morning or, as the unfriendly clerk informed me, I could take my daughter out of school. Wow. That just seemed outrageous. I then arrived at the post office at 10:05 a.m. on Saturday morning with both daughters, thinking we'll be in and out pretty quickly. An hour a half later we finally made it to the clerk. We then waited another 15 minutes as she clicked through all the pages on her screen. When we finally finished the process, I was left feeling robbed. My Saturday morning had been wasted in a totally unnecessary bureaucratic process.

This is an example of how bureaucracy can come to life in government at a local level, but it is also rife at the highest levels and can have a dramatic effect on a country's prosperity. Back in the late 1970s and early 1980s the New Zealand economy was crippled by far-reaching state bureaucracy and control. The government at the time controlled every part of the country. Prices were centrally controlled, there were limits on what you could earn, and you needed a license to import anything from overseas. Industries were heavily regulated and subsidized. To order a magazine or buy a car, you needed to apply for a permit, which usually would take a couple of months to process. This model was strangling the economy and crippling its competitiveness. By 1984 the economy was stagnating and close to failing. The government could not borrow any more money offshore, and there were upcoming payment deadlines that the government couldn't meet. Then the prime minister at the time, Robert Muldoon, called a snap election. His party lost and in came a new prime minister, David Lange, and a new finance minister, Roger Douglas. The country was in such a dire state that drastic change was required, and that's what the new government set about doing. Douglas rolled out a set of policies that sought to radically deregulate industries, lift controls, and crush bureaucracy. These policies became known as Rogernomics. Literally overnight, the extreme reach of the government was removed and the economy was opened to the world. Government agencies were drastically streamlined. Any role in any department that was considered to be producing busywork and not adding value was removed. The Forest Service went from having 17,000 employees to 17. The Department of Transportation went from having 5,600 employees to 53. Many state-owned enterprises were sold to the private sector. Bureaucratic practices and cumbersome legislation were removed. Taxes were simplified. All of a sudden there was a monumental shift away from anything that was overly complicated, added little value, and inefficient toward being open and lean and adding value. The government became streamlined, efficient, and focused on enabling and fostering a competitive economy. Obviously, this kind of change was traumatic, but highly necessary. People were forced to adjust and evolve. Innovation was now freed and people were encouraged to think and take ownership of their success.

Fast-forward 30+ years and New Zealand is regularly ranked as the most prosperous country in the world. Across various rankings New Zealand usually is within the top three for ease of doing business, least corruption, safest, and freest in the world. The country has the most innovative primary sector and is recognized as a hub for innovation and creativity. Local businesses are now so agile that if market conditions change offshore, they can immediately adjust to it. Without overbearing and burdensome controls and regulations, the country is primed to think, innovate, and create. It is clear that New Zealand's current success would not have been possible without the identification and removal of debilitating controls, processes, and bureaucracy.

One of the key areas that is impacted by bureaucracy is speed. Bureaucracy acts like an anchor, prohibiting efficiency and killing momentum. This can have important implications in certain contexts. US scientists have recently made a lot of progress on the field of gene editing. The technology named CRISPR-Cas9 acts like molecular scissors, enabling doctors to cut or repair DNA. The method can potentially be used to heal many ailments, including cancer. However, as it is a new technology and one that could have potentially harmful medical side effects, it has to go through regulatory review and gain approval. This clearly makes sense, as there have to be adequate testing and reviews to ensure safety prior to broadly rolling it out. The challenge is that the bureaucratic practices in agencies including the FDA results in the review period taking an exorbitant amount of time. The University of Pennsylvania, which has applied for the federal approval, have spent over two years addressing all of the federal requirements and still have not received clearance. In the meantime, the tool is being used in other countries where gaining regulatory approval is not so cumbersome. The tool has already reportedly helped numerous patients in counties, including China. This example demonstrates that while there is a role for regulatory intervention in certain industries, bureaucratic practices can inhibit access to potentially lifesaving technology for prolonged periods of time.

An important contributor to bureaucratic practices is unwieldy processes. Defining processes for how to complete organizational tasks has been bread-and-butter management or consultant work for decades. The genesis of process definition goes back as far as Frederick Taylor, who at the turn of the 20th century carefully observed his workers in an industrial setting and was able to define the steps they take to get the work done. This definition enabled him to explore and design new ways of organizing the steps to improve efficiency and productivity. Identifying better ways of doing a repeatable process has been a core management task for a long time and has delivered tons of value to businesses over the past century.

Given the attention that processes have received over the past century, it is no wonder that designing good processes has become a bit of an art form. Enter Six Sigma. There are actually belts in Six Sigma, like karate, given to those that achieve a certain level of process proficiency.

A couple of decades ago the school of Six Sigma was melded with another school called Lean. Lean is how organizations manage their businesses, with a strong cost-effectiveness orientation. It was a beautiful marriage between the process karate fighters and the cost-conscious bean counters. Their love child was Lean Six Sigma, which delivered a capability that built beautiful detailed processes that were guided by cost-effectiveness. The focus of this capability was on processes in the heart of manufacturing, distribution, and core back-office areas like finance, HR, and procurement.

The issue today is that the process wizards have gone a little too far. Everything within a business has been defined, organized, and broken down into a process. We have become engendered with a process orientation. As part of the 20th century organizational model of control, clear processes with associated roles and responsibilities meant that work could be controlled from high above. As discussed in the earlier chapter on structure, if people are forced to adhere to strict predefined processes, their brains check out and they lose the desire and ability to innovate. Over time, we also stopped questioning these processes. The clunky, unwieldy, and energy- and time-consuming processes became part of an organizational makeup. A great example is performance management.

Performance management is clearly an essential activity within organizations. But for decades the process of setting goals, both performance and development, referencing a detailed competency chart that is tied to levels and then going through the midyear and annual performance reviews, took an age to complete. The process was so clunky that people just wanted to get through it. The value of the activity was lost because people became too focused on just getting it done due to its time-consuming nature instead of focusing on the huge value it should deliver to an organization's workforce.

Then, around 2010, some authors and organizations began to question some of the core assumptions of performance management, such as the performance bell curve and ratings. This proved to be a catalyst for leaders to question whether their performance management processes were designed appropriately. When they reached out for feedback from their workforce, all of a sudden all the pain over the years of wasted time getting through this clunky process came out. Leaders, for the first time, realized that too much of their people's time and energy was being invested into a process that wasn't delivering an appropriate return. Consequently, performance management processes across the majority of organizations have been transformed over the past five to eight years.

At Simplify Work, we helped a large global fast food organization review and simplify their performance management approach. We helped them to better align their global competencies with their strategy so that people were building capabilities that would deliver the type of performance the company needed to win in the market. Also, we revealed where the greatest value in the performance management life cycle exists, which is in rich coaching conversations between leaders and their people. Getting clear on what is most important enabled disproportionate investment to be directed to those areas delivering greater value. We radically stripped away process steps and paperwork and grew a culture of ongoing rich coaching conversations. Given that coaching is not a natural skill for most people, heavy investment went into building this skill in managers. Now, instead of employees madly scrambling at the end of the year to complete their year-end review, schedule meetings with their managers/ team members, and receive/allocate a performance rating, performance conversations happen on an ongoing basis with performance proof points and key events being captured in the system throughout the year. This means that at the end of the year a performance discussion can be facilitated by referencing the content in the system and by more emphasis being put on looking forward to the exciting opportunities in the year ahead.

Examples of other processes that have become unwieldy and inappropriately time consuming include:

- **Budget setting:** The process is cumbersome, painful, and time consuming. It often requires multiple rounds of iterations and signoffs. It's especially time-consuming for those companies that use zero-based budgeting. Instead of leaning on the year before, each budget has to start from zero and justify each forecasted expense. It makes a lot sense in theory, as it is meant to keep an organization as lean as possible, but the problem is that in practice the process often becomes unwieldy and unnecessarily time-consuming.

- **Travel booking and expense processing:** In this day of significant cost controls, booking business travel is painful due to the multiple approvals required and ensuring adherence with strict cost parameters. Many conditions exist to drive costs down, like ensuring that travel is booked a certain number of weeks ahead or not spending over a certain limit on a hotel or food. There are also strict parameters on what can be expensed and what cannot. When a traveler returns, they then need to go through the time-consuming process of submitting their expenses and monitoring approval and reimbursement.

- **Keeping on top of compliance:** Ensuring that the workforce remains compliant and risk is managed appropriately can be another huge time suck for people. Some industries are more impacted by these requirements than others. Having worked at a large global accountancy, I can appreciate the amount of time required each year to keep up with compliance. There are likely many opportunities to streamline and enhance the way a workforce is kept in compliance. I remember clicking through the compulsory compliance e-learning screens as fast as I could; it felt like a big waste of time. Like the performance management example, the focus was on getting through a cumbersome, time-consuming process instead of focusing on the most important elements.

A useful exercise to do with your team or with your internal organization effectiveness group is to schedule a biannual or annual review of your core processes. Get clear on what your people spend their time on during the year, and then, as objectively as you can, explore the following questions for each process or activity:

- What value does this process deliver? How does this process positively impact the business?
- How many steps does is take to complete this process?
- How time-consuming is this process?
- What part of this process delivers the most value?
- Do we have the right people involved in this process?

- Is this process truly needed?

It will take courage to challenge embedded ways of working. People become used to the bureaucracy, so introducing change, even if it is common sense, can be met with resistance. There must be commitment from leadership and ideally a strong, clear strategic focus on simplification. This guiding light provides permission to question the status quo and reduce those things that don't deliver value. People are less likely to resist if they know the work is supporting a broader strategic initiative. As Steve Jobs said: "If you're ruled by processes, you don't need judgment—and I prefer judgment to process."[15]

While steps can be taken within functions and teams to reduce or remove low value processes or activities many companies have chosen to carve out chunks of repeatable process and move them to low-cost outsourced providers. It is now relatively common for Fortune 500 organizations to have shared service centers (SSCs) installed in low-cost locations. Typical destinations for this work include India, Central America (Costa Rica), Eastern Europe (Slovakia), and Southeast Asia (Philippines). One the challenges of moving to this model is that the level of service to employees diminishes due to the SSC staff operating in highly transactional ways, strictly adhering to established service level agreements. This often results in regular employees being left with more of an administrative burden, pulling them from more important work. I witnessed this at a large consumer packaged goods client. Moving swathes of back-office processes to regional shared service centers created more of a burden for staff as language barriers created conflict

---

15   Ken Segal, *Think Simple: How Smart Leaders Defeat Complexity* (Portfolio, 2016).

and the SSC's inability to be flexible on their service offerings resulted in local workarounds being created to avoid having to interact with the SSCs. While simply moving current processes to another provider may deliver cost savings, it can also increase complexity and consequently drive down productivity and engagement.

The reality today is that the vast majority of repeatable tasks will soon be automated. It is inevitable. Process by process, systems will increasingly take hold, automate, and digitize. It is a wonderful opportunity to review the role of humans in each of these mechanical processes. Interestingly, it will quickly put the global or regional SSC model at risk, as you'll have cloud-based software programs completing the work that the SSC folks used to do but much more efficiently and without mistakes as well as providing analytics where required. Watch this space.

Processes, rules, and other bureaucratic practices are common drivers of complexity and should be a target for simplification efforts. The more we can redesign or remove non-core, low-value activities and enable space and focus, the more likely we are to free the performance potential of people.

Making Sense of Systems

Too many employees struggle to find the information they need within their company's information systems. The technology boom over the past few decades has brought a software solution for everything. Thousands of IT companies trying to hawk their little piece of functionality to IT functions has resulted in organizations having a rich tapestry of systems that enable day-to-day operations. These beautiful system tapestries have created confusing labyrinths that people have to navigate through to get their job done. This ongoing day-to-day navigation wastes a significant amount of time and energy just to do core day-to-day tasks, such as:

- Find information on the various shared drives, intranet sites, and subsites or track down the person that has it on their hard drive.
- Remember your sixth user name and password to access the HR self-service program so that you can attempt to figure out how many vacation days you have left or your retirement contributions to date.
- Keep track of all the messages from the various communication platforms: Yammer, Slack, Google, WhatsApp, and Facebook.

I experienced this last example recently at a client. This large global organization of over 40,000 employees had a typical instant messenger function that was tied to their email application. Along with that was a clunky old tailored solution and then a number of public communication platforms that groups used to varying degrees throughout the global organization, including WhatsApp and country-specific platforms in China and India. In an effort to improve online collaboration, the company then rolled out Yammer, the Microsoft collaboration solution. The intent was laudable, but there was no plan for simplifying and consolidating the platforms in existence, so it simply added another communication vehicle to add to the confusion. My team was working on a global initiative to "crush complexity" at the time, so we noticed this development and tucked this opportunity under the wings of our effort. To help migrate various teams across the organization to Yammer and then encourage the sunsetting of the other collaboration tools, we had to carefully engage the right cheerleaders in each market. Leaders were tasked with increasing their presence on Yammer by contributing content, responding to conversations, and recognizing team members for excellent work. With commitment from leaders and effective awareness and reinforcement building via the global intranet, Yammer uptake significantly increased and online collaboration progressively became simplified.

A healthy way to assess system complexity is to take time biannually or annually to do a consumer review. Adhering to the design thinking methodology, put yourself in your users' shoes and try to understand their user experience by asking questions such as:

- How many systems do users need to interact with to get their job done?
- What are the most valuable pieces of information users need ready access to? How can priority information be accessed more easily?
- How can systems improve collaboration?
- How can we limit system enabled distractions and interruptions?
- How can we simplify the user interface across systems?

There is often a lot of opportunity with the last question. People don't want to have to click more than two or three times to get what they need. As part of a client's global operating model transformation where we led the change management, we at one point decided that the global function's intranet site was too 1997 and needed a design overhaul. From a change management perspective, we needed impacted stakeholders to have ready access to key information, and it was getting lost on their clunky intranet site. We brought in some system designers and overhauled the site. When reviewing all the subfolders, we discovered that there were pages of content that hadn't been updated for three years. There were subfolders and more subfolders. It was a maze of random content. With a view of the current structure and content, we took a step back and thought critically about what pieces of information people actually need. We also were realistic about what information topics could be kept up to date on an ongoing basis. We then collaborated around how to streamline the home page so that priority information became most easily accessible and navigation became simpler. We ended up reducing the number of subpages from 10 to four, and we stripped out words wherever we could and replaced them with simple images or didn't replace them at all. We installed a scrolling news feature and established a committee to keep the content updated on a weekly basis. Keeping it as simple as possible was our mantra and led to a 40% increase in activity in the three months following the release. We could now have more confidence that key transformation messages would be received and that people would gain a lot more value from the site.

With so much technology now, the challenge for CIOs and IT departments is how to deliver a streamlined, integrated, and, most importantly, simple experience to users. Large enterprise resource planning companies like Oracle and SAP have continued to acquire smaller leading system providers in an ongoing effort to deliver a simplified integrated system solution for organizations, but they can't keep up with the number of new software offerings being delivered almost weekly. So, any ambition to consolidate systems is almost mission impossible. Target has built their systems to be cloud agnostic so that applications can be designed without consideration of the underlying infrastructure, which saves time and enhances focus on the front-end design. It is easy to see that CIOs have an increasingly challenging task of connecting the tapestry of systems behind the scenes so that users do not have to click through 10 different systems to get their job done.

There are also opportunities to simplify and modernize the technology that drives key processes. One example is e-learning. Often, companies will have an intranet page dedicated to learning for a particular group that lists their e-learning content. This content is often a recorded PowerPoint presentation or one of those e-learning programs where you click on the screen to progress to the next screen. These training programs are often too long and just plain old boring. They do not drive usage or optimize learning. People want ongoing new content that is fresh and delivered in short video format. Companies are beginning to leverage the huge amount of free content available on platforms like YouTube or Khan Academy. Collaboration sites like Yammer allow people to share great content in their communities that they have come across and encourage people to take more ownership of their development. It also creates a viral movement toward learning cutting-edge content, skills, and methods, and not having to go through a clunky process of tracking down the right course, requesting attendance, scheduling it, and then attending. Instead, learning is constant, and emerging insights from various channels are funneled in a way that is engaging and time-effective. Learning resources can be redirected toward bringing people together in person for rich learning experiences that not only build new skills but also facilitate relationship building, which delivers value in a range of ways after training.

There will continue to be big opportunities for tech companies to create solutions to simplify the collection, analysis, and provision of data and insights. Even if there are many different systems operating in the background, IT functions need to deliver simple and user-friendly solutions for employees so the complexity is contained as much as possible and people get the right information or connectivity when they need it, in a form that is digestible and useable so that focus and energy can be used on problem solving and innovating.

Removing Counterproductive Cultural Traits

While it is essential that complexity is attacked at the strategic, structural, process, and system levels, it is also critical to attack it at the cultural level. Naturally, working in a particular fashion and adhering to certain processes and ways of working will create habits. These habits or routines across a group of people create a culture. And it is not realistic to flick the switch on structure and process and expect peoples' behaviors to immediately shift into line. Thus, a focus on culture and how to facilitate behavior change is an essential part of a simplification program.

Culture is a bit of nebulous topic. There are many different definitions and approaches for identifying and evolving culture. The well-known definition "the way we do things around here" is a pretty good way of capturing the essence of culture. I think once you realize that culture is simply the repeatable actions of a group of people, the concept becomes a little less fuzzy. The challenge, of course, is the task of changing the actions of a group of people in a particular way.

Cultures embody certain characteristics or traits. They come to life in particular styles of communicating, making decisions, and approaches to getting work done. Organizational cultures that promote debilitating complexity often possess the following characteristics or traits:

- **Management by committee:** Decisions are made by multiple individuals and consensus is required, slowing productivity.
- **Multiple checks and balances:** Decisions have to pass through multiple rounds of approvals, which inhibits speed and can discourage innovation.
- **Pursuit of perfection:** A strong desire to avoid mistakes leads to unnecessary overanalysis of every piece of work, resulting in wasted time.
- **Engage everyone:** Meetings are scheduled to keep broad stakeholder groups informed of work that is being completed, resulting in excessive low-value meetings that absorb time.
- **Cover-your-ass mentality:** People copy as many people as they can in email exchanges to ensure that they do not get in trouble, resulting in email overload.
- **Micromanagement:** Leaders and managers lean too far into the details of all work and feel the need to direct all activities, resulting in their people becoming transactional instruction followers.
- **Compliance obsession:** Being compliant becomes an obsession, which distracts focus from high-value activities that will actually benefit the business, like improving customer service or enhancing a product.
- **Intracompetitiveness:** The siloed nature of the organization creates intense competition across functions and groups, limiting effective collaboration.

I have witnessed these cultural traits in many of the clients I have worked with over the years. Often, people inside the organizations are well aware of the existence of the counterproductive working habits but feel paralyzed to do anything about it or are just unsure of where to start to change the culture. It can seem a little overwhelming when considering how to evolve how thousands or even tens or hundreds of thousands of people behave. Not surprisingly, the answer starts with getting simple.

A clear and simple mission or purpose can be an effective driver of people's behavior. If people know what their company stands for, it is a lot easier for them to act in accordance with it. A simple, compelling mission that is easily understandable and energizing will set the tone for how people should behave in every work setting.

Here are some great examples of simple and clear mission or purpose statements:

Ikea: To create a better everyday life for the many people

Apple Store: Enrich lives

Airbnb: Belong anywhere

Amazon: To be Earth's most customer-centric company, where people can find and discover anything they want to buy online

Google: Organize the world's information and make it universally accessible and useful

Microsoft: Empower every person and every organization on the planet to achieve more

Starbucks: To inspire and nurture the human spirit— one person, one cup and one neighborhood at a time

These short, punchy mission statements are often followed by a set of values that clarify the cultural guardrails. While many organizations have value statements that are not enforced and thus are meaningless, those that do take them seriously witness the impact it can have on a culture.

A good example is Whole Foods. Their mission is to only serve healthy food to their customers and they never waiver from this. They do not sometimes include brands that are "somewhat healthy"; they strictly adhere to their standards, which take into account artificial food preservatives, sustainable seafood, animal welfare, antibiotics in meat, and pesticides in vegetables. This commitment to the mission cascades through the organization and influences the way that all employees work on a daily basis.

Another example is at Simplify Work. Our mission is to improve lives through simplification. Each person on the team was selected partly based on their love of simplicity and the belief of the value it can deliver. The mission is supported by three values posed as questions that guide everything we do, from how we work together to how we create and deliver value for our clients. They are:

1. Can it be simpler?
2. Can it deliver more value?
3. Is it our best work?

If the mission and values are strong, leadership can let go of the reins of control. They can trust that their people will act in accordance with the mission and vision. Strong in-depth onboarding training that immerses new team members in the mission and values is often a good way of setting the tone early for new entrants. Various methods of reinforcement, such as storytelling and participative role modeling can be used during the immersion to bring to life what it means to work at a company. If the mission is clear and people understand and buy into it, the performance it can unleash can be dramatic.

David Marquet has created a great short YouTube video[16] in which he shares his direct experience in transforming the performance of his US Navy submarine crew by moving away from micromanagement and toward empowerment and autonomy. He did this in large part by setting clear expectations about how he wants people to work. These expectations were quite different from traditional navy leadership best practices but resulted in the performance of his crew growing exponentially to become the leading performing navy submarine. He did this by building a culture of ownership and empowerment. Instead of giving orders, Marquet clarified intent. If someone asked him, "What do I do, captain?" Marquet would respond with a question: "What do you think we should do given the current strategy or intent?" This got the crew thinking instead of blindly following instructions. Officers stopped requesting permission and took ownership of their area of responsibility. Marquet moved authority and decision making to where the information was in the organization. This meant that as a leader Marquet could focus on topline strategic thinking without

---

16   "Inno-Versity Presents: 'Greatness' by David Marquet," YouTube, October 8, 2013, https://youtu.be/OqmdLcyES_Q.

having to be involved in every decision and action. He no longer was a bottleneck. This shifted the culture from one that fostered blind instruction followers to a one that encouraged thinking, ownership, and innovation—which delivered significantly better performance.

Clarifying intent or a company's mission and values and then letting go of control is a great way to set your people free. But the rules have to be clear and unwavering. It makes me think back to the earlier example of society in general. We have laws, which establish a framework to live within. In most countries, we have the freedom to act, behave, and live in whatever way we want within the realm of the law. It's the same thing for organizations when they set their mission and guiding values. The mission and guiding values need to be clear, and the implications of breaking them need to be taken seriously.

The role of strong leadership in establishing a clear mission and values is essential. People look to leaders to guide their behavior, so the leaders need to carefully model the values they espouse. Often people learn the most from imitating the people they respect, so leaders really do need to walk the talk. But leaders can also play an active role in encouraging the removal of counterproductive cultural traits on an ongoing basis. Leaders should continue to reinforce the one or two things that really matter, thereby helping their teams to prioritize and focus. They should also help to remove roadblocks for their teams. When a counterproductive cultural trait rears its head, leaders should act quickly to snuff it out. Elon Musk did this at Tesla when he noticed that people were hesitant to reach out to people outside of their function due to concern about going around their bosses. He quickly sent out a memo clarifying his expectations and resetting cultural norms. The following was a companywide email from Musk[17]:

Subject: Communication within Tesla

There are two schools of thought about how information should flow within companies. By far the most common way is chain of command, which means that you always flow communication through your manager. The problem with this approach is that, while it serves to enhance the power of the manager, it fails to serve the company.

Instead of a problem getting solved quickly, where a person in one dept talks to a person in another dept and makes the right thing happen, people are forced to talk to their manager who talks to their manager who talks to the manager in the other dept who talks to someone on his team. Then the info has to flow back the other way again. This is incredibly dumb. Any manager who allows this to happen, let alone encourages it, will soon find themselves working at another company. No kidding.

Anyone at Tesla can and should email/talk to anyone else according to what they think is the fastest way to solve a problem for the benefit of the whole company. You can talk to your manager's manager without his permission, you can talk directly to a VP in another dept, you can talk to me, you can talk to anyone without anyone else's permission. Moreover, you should consider yourself obligated to do so until the right thing happens. The point here is not random

---

17   Justin Bariso, "This Email from Elon Musk to Tesla Employees Describes What Great Communication Looks Like," Inc.com, August 30, 2017, https://www.inc.com/justin-bariso/this-email-from-elon-musk-to-tesla-employees-descr.html, accessed December 5, 2017.

chitchat, but rather ensuring that we execute ultra-fast and well. We obviously cannot compete with the big car companies in size, so we must do so with intelligence and agility.

One final point is that managers should work hard to ensure that they are not creating silos within the company that create an us vs. them mentality or impede communication in any way. This is unfortunately a natural tendency and needs to be actively fought. How can it possibly help Tesla for depts to erect barriers between themselves or see their success as relative within the company instead of collective? We are all in the same boat. Always view yourself as working for the good of the company and never your dept.

Thanks,

Elon

This kind of strong leadership plays an important role in stripping out counterproductive ways of working and helps to keep simplification front and center.

There are also other ways of stripping out counterproductive cultural traits. It helps to start with getting very clear on what the current culture actually is—the good, the bad, and the ugly. Getting clear on the current culture enables clarity on what to do less of but also what aspects of the current culture should be retained and strengthened going forward. No culture is all bad, and so it is important to retain and strengthen those pieces of culture that embody the positive ethos of an organization. An aspired culture can be defined as a set of characteristics or traits that embody both old and new elements. These elements should be translated into specific actionable behaviors. This list, which is normally pretty long, is then distilled into a set of two to four behaviors that will have the greatest impact on attaining the desired cultural evolution. This helps to focus the effort, as attempting to get a group to adopt a laundry list of 20 behaviors will never work. This set of core or critical behaviors should then be widely communicated and reinforced through a number of channels and tactics. One of the most powerful techniques in sharing and fostering commitment to the critical behaviors is recruiting highly respected individuals across the business to be cheerleaders. It can be tricky to track down these authentic mentors, but once you do and you have them on board with the effort, it can fuel a viral movement that can take on a life of its own. Another effective method of reinforcing desired ways of working is to have quirky prizes or awards for those demonstrating the desired behaviors. Amazon is known for giving out a highly coveted "door desk award," which looks like a regular desk and is awarded to those that come up with great new ideas like how to "better affix shipping labels to packages and how to save money on conference room equipment."[18] This award reinforces a behavior that Amazon cherishes: the constant pursuit of better.

The traditional thinking in changing culture is that you should change the way someone thinks, then how they feel and then how they act. This approach actually doesn't work very well, as it is very difficult to change someone's mindset. The better approach is to act your way into new thinking, which Jon Katzenbach and his colleagues discuss in their article "10

---

18   Vanessa Fuhrmans and Yoree Koh, "The 250 Most Effectively Managed U.S. Companies—and How They Got That Way," *Wall Street Journal*, December 6, 2017, https://www.wsj.com/articles/the-most-effectively-managed-u-s-companiesand-how-they-got-that-way-1512482887, accessed December 6, 2017.

Principles of Organizational Culture."[19] Being very clear on the new actions people should take makes it easier for them to try to repeat a new way of doing something, and then new habits and routines naturally take hold, which will eventually shift one's mindset.

Neuroscience research backs up this approach. The more you think and act in a particular way, the more you are strengthening a neural pathway in your brain. This is essentially habit building. It actually feels good when you follow an embedded routine, as you don't have to expend much energy. If you travel frequently for work, think about how when catching an early morning flight, you can shower, shave, and dress on automatic pilot. When I was a consultant traveling weekly, the whole Monday morning routine was so second nature that it was only when I had my first cup of coffee when my flight landed that I really woke up.

When dealing with a deluge of information, it is simpler for the brain to repeat an existing blueprint—or neurological pathway—than build a new one. In a highly complex environment where employees are constantly pulled in many directions and have too many things to complete simultaneously, their capacity to think and create in original ways is significantly impaired. In short, your brain likes to stick to what it knows.

Doing something or learning something totally new is quite exhausting. I remember feeling this way after the all-day training sessions I would attend at the big consulting houses.

---

19   Jon Katzenbach, Carolin Oelschlegal, and James Thomas, "10 Principles of Organizational Culture," *Strategy + Business*, February 15, 2016, https://www.strategy-business.com/feature/10-Principles-of-Organizational-Culture, Accessed September 20, 2017.

The level of exhaustion would also correlate with the style of learning: if there was a lot of reading text versus watching video and engaging in activities, it would be a much more exhausting experience.

Another piece of neuroscience research that applies to the role of culture in reducing complexity is sustaining brain performance. To maximize performance, our brain needs to experience a state of relative excitement. If we do not experience intellectual excitement, the brain's capacity to think creatively exponentially diminishes over time. When employees are mired in complex and controlling processes, rules, and systems, their capacity to think creatively not only is reduced in the present but diminishes further over time. I have witnessed this firsthand with many clients I have worked with over the years.

From banks to consumer goods clients, I've witnessed companies full of employees that have been in the same role for a decade at least, often a lot longer, and are very comfortable following the same routine day in and day out. Their ability to think outside the box doesn't exist without significant coaxing. Often these clients' offices reflect this entrenched complacency. One of my clients used to have a stodgy old campus in a distant Chicago suburb, and walking into the place felt like stepping into a time warp to 1984. It was cubicle country with lovely beige carpet that hadn't been updated since Skid Row was on the charts. Most employees had been in their roles for decades and were coming in and simply going through the motions each day. It was clear that the employees had long given up on trying something different due to the crippling bureaucracy and politics. They would sit in their cubicles and plan their next vacation. They were checked out. It is understandable that when a new CEO was brought in to transform the organization and offered a voluntary severance package, a significant proportion of the employee population decided to take it. They didn't have the energy for or interest in going through any hard changes that would result in them having to work differently. This point also shows the interesting effect that a physical environment can have on culture and on contributing to debilitating complexity.

In the early 2000s, office designers started to blow up the traditional crowded office space for more open-plan offices. This movement certainly was an improvement in many respects; it brought people together more, which fostered more informal knowledge sharing, and the open space and increased natural light supported creativity. However, the one thing that probably wasn't taken into account was the rise in interruptions and distractions that this office design would fuel. It takes energy and time to get into a state of focused concentration, and when it is broken by an unexpected interruption, it can take some time to regain this productive state. So an open office without quiet spaces can actually have a negative effect on productivity. Some companies have learned from this and have configured spaces in their offices for people to have uninterrupted focus time or to simply switch off for a little while. They encourage their people to take time to get away from the constant requests and information overload and take time to recharge their batteries. Companies including Google, Facebook, and Amazon (all big tech firms) have created these types of spaces. Employees can use these spaces to meditate, reflect, or even take a power nap. These spaces are important symbols to employees. It tells them that their company cares about their well-being. In return, employees feel engaged and are more likely to give more of themselves to the organization.

Other companies also use their physical space to foster a productive and engaged culture. The colors on the walls, picture choice, lighting, open spaces, and natural light all influence workers' mental state. Increasingly, top companies are bringing in office environment designers to help create optimal spaces to foster productive, engaged, and innovative teams. A challenge that some companies are facing is the trend of more of their employees working remotely. These individuals would obviously not get the benefit of working in the carefully designed spaces. This is an emerging opportunity space for further investigation.

Culture is a big topic that can be influenced by many things from a clear mission to leadership communications to physical spaces. One thing is certain: culture is an essential ingredient in simplifying an organization and should be equally weighted with structure, process, and system simplification. While it is not easy to change culture, it can be achieved with a focused effort and be a critical driver of simplifying work.

CHAPTER 4

Simplify You

The "overwhelmed employee"[20] has received a lot of attention over the past few years. People have more and more work to do and are struggling to keep up with it all. People are spending less and less time with their families and not taking time to disconnect, switch off, and recharge. It has become quite hard to disconnect when we have constant access to our email, social networking sites, news, and other sources of distraction. Work is also becoming increasingly global which requires being "on" at times normally spent working out or with family.

---

20   Juliet Bourke, "The Overwhelmed Employee: Simplify the Work Environment," Deloitte.com, https://www2.deloitte.com/au/en/pages/human-capital/articles/overwhelmed-employee-simplify-environment.html.

The issue is that we lose sight of what is truly most important when we run from one thing to the next. The go-go-go mindset reduces one's ability to think strategically and operate in a proactive manner. We feel that to be more successful, generate more revenue, or achieve that goal we simply need to do more. It doesn't help that when we do deliver a great product or project we're rewarded with more work. Many of us actually consider being busy a badge of honor. But the reality is that we have so much going on and are pulled in so many directions that we are left feeling overwhelmed and close to burning out. We wake up one morning and realize that years have passed in a haze of deadlines and conference calls. We've missed out on critical experiences with our kids, and we've lost touch of our true passions.

Here are some of the typical things I have heard from those in my network that are run ragged:

- I feel unhealthy. I don't have time to make proper food, get enough sleep, or work out.
- The emails are constant. I feel like my phone is a vibrator that can't be switched off.
- If I can just get through this next project I'll have some breathing space.
- I just can't keep up with all the firefighting.

I'm obviously painting a pretty dismal picture, but there is hope! While we can't escape the reality of 21st-century business, steps can be taken and skills can be built to smash complexity in your life, take control, increase your energy, be more productive, and be generally happier. It's time to begin to live simply.

Here are steps you can take to simplify you:

1. Reduce clutter.
2. Get clear on what is most important.
3. Plan effectively.
4. Avoid distractions and interruptions.
5. Optimize email and meetings.
6. Nurture and protect your energy.

Reduce Clutter

Let's start with reducing clutter. We have become hoarders of stuff. Both professionally and personally, we retain too many things and let our lives become cluttered. We may not realize it, but all of this stuff weighs on our mind and contributes to a sense of losing control. A good first step in simplifying you is taking the time to declutter and reorganize. It is mentally liberating when we get rid of all the things that are not needed. It simplifies our environment, which subconsciously makes us feel less stressed and mentally scattered.

I am a father of two young girls, and thus keeping clutter-free is hard. It's so easy to accumulate stuff from toys, puzzles, books, strollers, scooters, and so on. My wife and I celebrate every time we can get rid of something we no longer need. There was a big high-five when we could sell the high chair. We recently gave away the double stroller, and the next big item on the list is the changing table. I think a cork will be popped when that one is gone. It takes discipline and focus to keep your world clutter-free, but the mental freedom it delivers is well worth it.

A good place to start is your desk. Many of us with messy desks believe that it is "organized chaos" and that we know where everything is. The reality is that having to keep tabs of all the documents – notes, to-dos, contracts, and so on is mentally taxing. Installing a system to manage your desk and keep it clear gives you an important shot of focus and releases energy that can be used to do something productive.

Carve out an hour or two and review all the pieces of paper on your desk. Ask yourself of every piece of paper: "What do I need to know or do with this paper?" "When was the last time I used this content?" You may think that you'll need some of the content at some point in the future, but I would encourage you to be bold and discard anything that is not really worth retaining. With all the documentation create three discrete piles:

Pile 1: To be thrown out
Pile 2: To be actioned and then thrown out
Pile 3: To be filed for future reference

Once all paper is accounted for, retain the things that stimulate you, calm you, and motivate you. Pictures of your family or images of a beautiful natural landscape are good options as they are soothing, inspiring, and a source for happiness. You could have some self-affirmations or motivational quotes from someone you respect. All of this serves to fuel your productivity and focus.

Once your desk is clutter-free, you may have a few documents that need to be filed. Physical filing can take a little time. I was one of those people that used to put things off that weren't a priority, like tidying up a filing cabinet. I also retained documentation I thought may be of use in the future. When I eventually carved out a morning to reorganize and declutter my filing cabinet, it was a big day. Once you get into it and start throwing things away, it immediately starts to feel good. You easily find yourself in declutter mode and the momentum will build. Really question whether you will actually get use out of each document in the future. Based on experience, 85% of documentation you retain you won't use again. So, the 15% of the information you actually need is being lost in all the other 85%. Be ruthless. We keep far too many documents. I would hate to see on average over a year how much time is wasted looking for documents we need. I'm sure it would be weeks. Needless to say, simplifying file structures and culling unneeded material will have a big impact on your productivity.

Take time to also consolidate and streamline your folder titles. Try to create mutually exclusive folders; any folders that could be combined should be. I integrated professional articles I wanted to keep with other business forms that I couldn't throw away, like business identification forms. I used to have a file full of physical articles or PowerPoint decks I added to over the years. I also kept all official documentation I received for Simplify Work, like insurance information and bank notifications. I realized that the vast majority of this content did not need to be retained, and I was able to merge two folders into one, given the significantly reduced size of them.

There may be a few pieces of information in certain documents that is worth keeping a record of, in which case you can pull those bits of information and capture them in an electronic file. Which brings us to computer files. These certainly should not escape our decluttering rampage.

Use the afternoon to review your computer files and delete duplications and low-value files of every sort. Consolidate folders as much as possible and again, remove any that you don't need. The goal is getting to a streamlined folder structure with contents that you actually use. If there are files that you truly believe are worth retaining but will not likely use on an ongoing basis, move them from your hard drive to a dedicated folder on an external hard drive or in the cloud. Free up and simplify your hard drive. When I reviewed my old folder structure, I had 10 folders with numerous subfolders. Within each subfolder were tons of documentation I had incrementally added over the years. It took some time but after the decluttering process I now have six folders with streamlined subfolders, now holding far fewer documents. I now can find information I need much easier, saving me time and energy every day.

Don't forget about the cloud, either. It has become the new dumping ground for all our "might use at some point" material. Due to the massive capacity of our cloud accounts, we are tempted to dump anything of interest there. The problem is that our cloud accounts are becoming totally cluttered with various photos, music, and random documentation. Follow the same system as you did with your filing cabinet and hard drive; remove anything that isn't really of use and streamline your folder structure.

All of a sudden, at the end of the day you will find that you have a clear desk, a thinned out filing cabinet, and an organized and streamlined folder structure on both your hard drive and cloud account. There will also be a big pile of trash on the floor to discard. And it will feel great! It will feel like a weight has been lifted. Your newfound conversion to the declutter tribe will likely motivate you to look at other parts of your house or life. You may want to review your book collection. I found I didn't use or need about 70% of my books, so decided to donate all the excess to a local used book store. I also went into my closet and looked at all of my clothes and shoes. There were so many shirts, T-shirts, and pants that I never wear or may wear once a year. I got a big garbage bag and with my decluttering zeal set about filling the bag with any item of clothing that I didn't really need. Like my excess books, it felt good to be able to donate my excess clothing to the Salvation Army. Now when I visit a clothing store and I see something that may look good, I really question whether I actually need it. It is a mindset shift that enables me to retain by decluttered status and saves money in the process.

While it may seem challenging to find the time to declutter, it is certainly worth the investment. It is a valuable step toward taking control of your life and gaining the individual clarity that seems to be out of reach for most in today's high-paced, scattered world. There really is something to be said for the minimalism movement that seems to be taking hold in many parts of the world.

Get Clear on What Is Truly Important

One of the major issues with seemingly too much work and operating in a reactive, firefighting mode is that you lose focus on what is most important. Your time is spent on relatively lower-value activities as you get caught up reacting to requests or the latest issue. Your impact on the business is diminished, and it can seem hard to break free from it. Getting clear on what is most important, those things that will deliver the greatest impact on the business, will allow you to free yourself from the chains of reactive working and take control over your time and focus.

Take some time to answer the following questions:

- What is the purpose of my role?
- How can I add the most value to the business?
- What are the most productive and impactful activities I do?
- How do I produce the best work?

- What do I need to produce my best work?

To uncover the answers to some of these questions, you will need to have a clear understanding of your business. You will need to have a strong grasp of your company's strategy and what capabilities they need to build or strengthen, what products or services they need focus on, and what markets to enter or expand their footprint in. With this understanding, a clearer connection can be made between how your role can have the greatest positive impact on the business' performance.

With the answers to these questions you can begin to distill your professional priorities. The answers will reveal what activities and projects will have the greatest impact on the business and therefore your performance. It should also reveal how you can be most effective at delivering these most important things.

Make sure that your newfound priorities are aligned with the people that you work with, including your team, manager, and peers. With alignment with these key stakeholders you now have permission to take control of how you get the most valuable work done. You can now turn off the low-value and distracting noise that used to consume your time. With clarity on what truly matters most you can say no to the various requests that bubble up during a normal day. You can avoid being sucked into seemingly endless email chains that never get resolved quickly due to the 20 people copied on them. You can decline requests to attend meetings that you don't really need to be a part of. Anything that takes up your time that could be better spent on your highest priorities should go by the wayside or moved to Friday afternoon.

Another area in which to gain clarity on what is most important is your personal life. Gaining clarity on the most important things in your world will help you to better plan and allocate your time so you're not only delivering significant impact at work but also on things outside of work, like your family, health, spirituality, and other interests.

I attended a leadership development program while a consultant at Booz & Company. The week-long program was held among the beautiful red cliffs of Sedona, Arizona. On day 3 we did an interesting exercise on personal values. We each received a deck of cards, and each card in the pack had a value on it such as integrity, health, entrepreneurship, family, and so on. Our job was to sort through the pack and put each card into three piles: most important, moderately important, and less important. Once you got through the pack of cards and had your three piles, you then had to sort through your most important pile to get to your top five values. This is actually a lot harder than you think, especially if you're taking the exercise seriously. There was a lot of reflection and pondering going on, but eventually we all landed on our five. We then drew a picture on a flip chart to illustrate our five top values. It was a powerfully impactful exercise; the vast majority of people in the room had never stopped and spent time to honestly reflect on what is truly most important to them before. This group of elite strategy consultants were typical type-A, hard-charging, hypercompetitive types who never paused to reflect and think about their bigger picture. Their focus for such a long time had been on how quickly they could achieve the next promotion. This exercise exposed some hidden truths that would examine their reality. Many realized that their most important values in their life were things like family, health, autonomy, spirituality, and so on. The obvious intuitive next question was: "Are you living in accordance with your core values?" The answer for the vast majority was no. They were working extremely long hours, traveling most of the week, eating out every night, and not having time to work out. Gaining this clarity on what is truly most important was a profound revelation and led to at least 30% of the class deciding to leave the firm to pursue something that would be more in line with the things they care most about.

I have since used this same exercise in leadership development programs we have delivered, and it continues to have the same effect on people. But you don't necessarily need to go to the extreme of quitting your job to live in alignment with both your professional and personal priorities. You just need to learn to plan properly.

Plan Effectively

Effective planning can serve to keep you focused on what matters most, both professionally and personally. It breaks down how top goals will be achieved and carves out time to be spent on personal priorities like family and health. But it requires discipline to stick with the cadence and not get pulled away from the structure.

Let's start with the levels of planning. You can break down your planning process into annually, quarterly, and weekly.

Annually

The planning process begins with an annual plan. This is obviously very macro as you formulate the broad objectives for the year ahead. Most companies have a formal annual goal-setting process where individuals develop their goals for the year ahead with the company's strategy informing the process.

This is normally done at the beginning of the year and in some cases takes three to four months to complete and get signoff. The biggest disconnect with the traditional goal planning process is the lack of ongoing planning on quarterly, monthly, and weekly bases. Without the continuity in planning, it becomes far too easy to lose sight of the key goals and to become reactive to everyday demands.

An important strategy with annual planning is to start by melding your professional and personal goals so you have a comprehensive view of your goals. I think of the traditional "balanced scorecard" that some companies use to broaden how they measure the performance of their business. Rather than simply focusing on financial performance, using a balanced scorecard measures performance across other categories including "customer," "learning and growth," and "internal processes." This view provides more of an indication of an organization's health. In using this method to meld professional and personal goals you can distill and combine goals to establish a broader view, such as:

- **Professional:** Launch the Organization Effectiveness Center of Excellence.
- **Professional:** Get promoted to VP.
- **Health:** Complete a triathlon. Attend touch rugby nationals competition.
- **Family:** Establish Sunday as a family day. Take girls to school twice a week.
- **Relationships:** Establish weekly date night with wife.

The breakdown will look very different for each person. There are varying levels of detail to be included, but it is important to be as specific and measureable as possible. I would encourage you to sit down with your partner to talk through your personal balanced scorecard. Once you're comfortable with your melded goals, then you can lean into the details of your professional goals, which will likely be determined by your company's performance management program.

I find that over the year-end break I naturally find myself reflecting on the achievements of the last year, which then shifts into formulating goals for the year ahead. I find that this is a healthy process, especially if you are able to take some time away from your usual location. Getting away often stimulates reflection and fuels the process of considering what's most important in the year ahead, both professionally and personally. So, if you can, take some time away at the end of the year and lean into the crafting of your annual balanced scorecard.

Quarterly

Annual goals should be broken down into quarterly objectives. Each quarter, there should be specific goals for each category of your personal balanced scorecard. There could be goals like sell four consulting projects and teach my daughter how to fly fish. At the end of each quarter there needs to be a careful review of your performance. If the goals are crafted in a specific and measureable fashion, it makes the review process a lot more objective and less subjective. These reviews should occur not only with your teams and leaders within the company but also with your significant other (if you have one). These conversations should be real but also constructive. One of the major issues with traditional performance management is that the focus is too much on what was not achieved so the experience is a very negative one. People participating in this type of performance review naturally dread having them, and the value of the exercise is lost. A better approach is to focus on recognizing achievements made and inviting self-reflection on goals not met by asking the right questions. If the person who is being reviewed feels like they have the support and encouragement of the reviewer, they feel energized and motivated to pursue the development opportunities. Rather than leave these important conversations feeling depressed and stressed, people feel empowered and positively charged.

A lot of things can change in a quarter on both business and personal fronts. The company could decide to reorganize or acquire another company. There could be competitive moves, new technology, or radically shifting consumer preferences. All of these developments could likely affect you and your role, so you may need to evolve your annual goals. There could also be changes for you personally, like a family member passing away, a health problem, or a sports opportunity presents itself. The quarterly review provides you with the opportunity to reset your annual goals.

Quarterly planning enables focus to be retained on what is most important for you, professionally and personally. The output of this level of planning should drive the next level of planning: weekly planning.

Weekly

At the end or the beginning of each week take time to set a few specific objectives for the week ahead. With your quarterly goals in mind, craft a list of specific actionable goals. These goals can include both professional and personal goals and could include goals such as "Make 10 sales calls per day" or "Get eight hours of sleep per night." But while they can be either professional and personal, they should be measureable.

Each person has their own preference of doing weekly planning on a Friday or a Monday. I find doing it on a Friday afternoon works well because it reduces the risk that you'll worry about what's coming up in the week ahead while you're trying to enjoy personal time over the weekend. I will then review the list first thing on a Monday and may make tweaks. It's helpful to put the list somewhere where you can see it so that you continue to get reminders of what's most important during the week. A Post-it page is one good option or simply having the list on a piece of paper that you leave on your desk where you can readily see it. I use the sticky note feature on my laptop desktop so I see my weekly goals every time I start up my laptop or shut it down. My annual and quarterly goals are listed there as well.

Once you have your weekly goals, you need to plan your week around achieving them. This is where your calendar plays an integral role. You should be living by your calendar. You should hold sacred the time you carve out in your calendar. For instance, if you know that you'll need to collaborate with two other people as part of a solution design process, ensure that you block out appropriate time in your calendar not only to attend the session but also to prepare for it and to synthesize the output. You may also need to build out a particular deliverable. Again, block time in your calendar, preferably when you are at your most productive, so that you can focus on getting this important piece of work completed. Also, and importantly, plug in time to accomplish your personal goals. If you like to swim in the morning, block time for this activity. If you pick your child up from school twice a week, block this time in your calendar. I even include things outside business hours. My weekly date nights are in there. My weekend activities are in there. I find it helps me keep alignment with my wife on what personal commitments we have. Being disciplined with translating planning into blocking time in your calendar will enable you to better achieve your most important goals. It will also reduce the risk that you get distracted, which is one of the major contributors to goals not being achieved.

Avoid Distractions and Interruptions

How often do you check your phone? The average person does it 110 times a day,[21] and this number is increasing all the time. Our smartphones have become so magnetic. We feel a constant pull from our phones to check if anyone has emailed us or liked or commented on a photo or a recent post, or to keep up on the latest news or sports scores. This addiction to our phones is massively distracting and interruptive and gets in the way of us producing our best work. It used to be the little red light from our Blackberry that resulted in us incessantly checking our phones, but now it is a little beep or a vibration of our smartphone. With the invention of smart watches we now can't escape the interruptions as we receive a vibration on the wrist any time an email, text message, or app update is received. With advancing technology there is an increasing number of sources of distraction and interruption.

Every time we are interrupted or distracted it breaks any concentration we may have been trying to cultivate. When our

---

21   Victoria Woollaston, "How Often Do You Check Your Phone? The Average Person Does It 110 Times a Day (and up to Every 6 Seconds in the Evening," DailyMail.com, October 8, 2013, http://www.dailymail.co.uk/sciencetech/ article-2449632/How-check-phone-The-average-person-does-110-times-DAY-6-seconds-evening.html.

focus is broken our productive energy is wasted and it takes time and energy to get focus back. It is also so easy to get pulled into the thing that has interrupted you. You see a notification that someone has liked a LinkedIn article you have posted, so you go to see who it was. Once there, you see that there are other updates and one of your former colleagues has published an interesting new article. You decide to read it. On and on, one thing leads to another, and before you know it you've wasted an hour of your time that could have been spent working toward your highest priorities.

There is a difference between a distraction and an interruption. A distraction is something that pulls your attention. It could be an interesting article you have up on your web browser waiting for you to read it while you're attempting to build an important PowerPoint slide. It could be a television screen within eyeshot with an interesting show or news article playing while you're trying to keep focused on your laptop. An interruption is something that breaks your concentration. It could be an instant messenger icon popup with a message from one of your colleagues. It could someone walking into your office or someone talking loudly in your open-plan office space. Distractions and interruptions have become prolific in modern day companies and are a major barrier to productivity and innovation.

I believe in the coming years that there will be a backlash against the constant interruptions that technology enables. I believe that as more people come to realize that rich innovation comes from unbroken focus or as people begin to value uninterrupted quality time with their family, they will choose products that enable and promote quiet periods. But in the interim every tech company will continue to scramble to capture and hold our attention for as long as they can. They will continue to build pesky notifications that tease us with content that we find hard to ignore.

To help simplify work and optimize our productivity and impact we need to have the discipline to not be tempted by our magnetic technology products. But you can make it easy on yourself by taking a few deliberate steps to remove or reduce the risk that our focus is broken during our productive times.

- Turn off all notifications on your smartphone. Go into the settings and turn off each notification associated with your email and for each application.
- If you're not using it, switch it off. Any time you're not using an application or internet page on your computer, exit out of it. The more things you have up in your computer, the more scattered you will feel and the more risk there is that you'll get pulled from the most important work. According to one study, 57% of interruptions at work resulted from either social media tools or switching among disparate stand-alone applications.
- Schedule productive time on your calendar. During this period exit out of your email and enable the do not disturb function on instant messenger. Close all non-core applications on the computer. This means no internet. Turn off your phone or put it in do not disturb mode. And, if need be and you have a private office, inform your colleagues that if your door is closed you do not want to be disturbed.
- Allocate time for everything else. Schedule breaks on your calendar when you can catch up on your social

media platforms, read up on the latest news, or engage in banter with your colleagues.

Make it easier on yourself to truly focus and produce your best work by simplifying your environment and turning off interruptions, notifications, and distractions. In addition to scheduling time to do your best work, schedule time to check in on all the platforms that you like. I usually use the time just before or after lunch to check my personal email, trawl through LinkedIn, or check in on Facebook. During lunch, if I'm not meeting someone, I'll review the day's news headlines by reading articles or watching a news channel. Allocating time for interruptions and distractions not only protects your productive time but also enables you to recharge your batteries throughout the day.

Optimize Email and Meetings

Email overload plays a big part in our sense of being overwhelmed. We spend big chunks of our day trying to respond to all of the emails but struggle to keep up with them all. All of this time spent dealing with emails results in limited time to do other important activities, like collaborating on a high-priority initiative or meeting with key customers. Also, feeling the need to respond quickly to all emails means that your focus is broken anytime an email is received. It doesn't help when leaders have an expectation on receiving a response to their emails within 30 minutes. When I was consultant at Booz & Company, I certainly knew of many partners that were so inclined. They would expect an immediate response to their emails, and if they didn't receive one they would email again and then after five minutes had passed they would call. This naturally creates a culture of email anxiety, and anytime your phone vibrates you rapidly stop everything to check it to see if it needs an immediate response. When I left Booz & Company, it took me a good four months to shake the habit of immediately reacting to my phone vibrating. I still occasionally find myself doing it from time to time.

To take control of your time and productivity, there are better ways for managing emails. These can be distilled into three tactics:

1. Set times to deal with email.
2. One touch = one action
3. Reset expectations on email inclusivity.

A good strategy for avoiding email interruptions and increasing email productivity is carving out specific times in the day to review and deal with emails. This means that emails do not interrupt our productivity and creative juices. You may need to set the expectation with your colleagues that you will get to their email at a certain time so that they know not to expect an immediate response. Some go as far as to use an autoresponder that is immediately replies to the sender, informing them that they should expect a response within two days. Like checking in on social networking sites and other distractions, I find that dealing with email is a good activity either just before or after lunch and then again at the end of the day. This leaves quality time in the morning and afternoon to allocate to the highest-priority work.

The second strategy for better managing email is one touch = one action. How many times do you handle an email before you deal with it? Do you read it and come back to it later? Do you wish you didn't have so many unopened emails? Multiple handling of an email is a big, unnecessary time suck. A better approach is to deal with the email as soon as you open it. Do I respond, do I delete, or do I unsubscribe? If you can respond to an email within 10 minutes, do it there and then. Delete those that don't require action. And unsubscribe from those that you shouldn't have received. Schedule time in your calendar to respond to emails that require some work or time to respond to, and come back to them then.

Also, set up a logical and simple folder or tagging system in your email. One of the key tactics used to simplify is organization. This applies to emails as well. Organizing emails will help you make sense of the laundry list of emails and enable you to prioritize your time on the most important topics.

The third strategy for better managing email is resetting expectations on inclusivity. Inclusiveness is currently a corporate hot topic and a worthy one, but it shouldn't influence email etiquette. The ridiculous quantities of email that many people have to deal with is partly to do with a highly inclusive email culture. Some companies have cultures where everyone is copied on everything. This is normally due to people wanting to cover their ass so that someone who could be peripherally connected or impacted does not get upset if they find out about the online conversation. A better, simpler approach is to copy people sparingly. Only copy those who are directly involved in the work and could respond. If the focus is on the work and not on protecting your fiefdom, there shouldn't be adverse reactions to someone entering your turf without consent. Some leaders do not even take time to read emails that they are copied on. This is extreme but may be necessary for those who receive over 100 emails per day.

A similar problem is including everyone in meeting invitations. Low-value meetings are the biggest source of wasted time in organizations today. One of my clients has an "engage everyone" culture. Not only was I invited to meetings that should have been emails, but the meetings went on for far too long. The hour-long meetings could have been 20 minutes in most cases. As the owner of your productivity, you need to be confident enough to say no to meeting requests that are not worth your time. You never know, your act of saying no may set off a movement and shift the meeting culture.

But don't stop there. Why not lead the charge in leading effective meetings? Set clear agendas with clear expected outcomes. Send out material to be reviewed prior to the meeting and set the expectation that it won't be covered during the meeting. This way people can come to the meeting clear on their role and the expected outcomes and can dive into the most valuable activities: collaboration, problem solving, and decision making.

Nurture and Protect Energy

Energy is an emerging focal area in organizational effectiveness and an important component of simplification. I'm not talking about oil and gas, but individual human energy. In this digital era, when we have constant access to everything and everyone has constant access to us, we have lost sight of the importance of nurturing and directing our energy in deliberate ways. Being always on is now the new norm with LinkedIn, Facebook, email, and various app notifications pinging us constantly and breaking our focus. Each time we are interrupted and our deep concentration is broken, it uses energy. We also are expected to keep charging at work, often without breaks, and retain our optimal levels of productivity. It's no wonder that we have become coffee and energy drink fiends. Any time we feel our concentration dropping we head on over to the coffee machine and fill 'er up. And then we wonder why we don't seem to have quality sleep any more. We also let stress consume us. But we don't realize the long-term effects of constantly being in a haze of negative emotions.

There are better, more sustainable methods of managing and optimizing our energy. *Mindfulness* is a buzzword that has become quite popular over the past few years. Being mindful is essentially being present in the moment, not focused on what is coming up, like a critical corporate event or a vacation. Being in the present enables clarity of mind and reduces stress and anxiety for things that have not yet happened. It also encourages appreciation of the now, which is a major driver of happiness. It may seem like I'm becoming a little philosophical, but there is power in some of these techniques that have been around for thousands of years.

Mediation is a great exercise for being mindful and fully aware in the moment, and it is increasingly being used in the corporate world. Just practice sitting still in a preferably quiet place and direct your focus to your breath. Straighten your back, relax your shoulders and your face, and keep focusing on your breath. Actively let all of the noise in the front of your brain quiet, and let go of all the things on your to-do list and any concerns you may have. If your mind drifts and you start to think about an email you need to write, bring it back to the present. If you have no experience meditating, you'll likely find it very difficult to keep your focus on your breath and the present, but the more you bring it back and focus on quieting your brain, the more you'll slip into deep meditation. Only a few minutes in a meditative state is hugely energizing. When you emerge from only five minutes of meditating, you'll find that your perspective has shifted. You're no longer mentally grappling with all the things that need to get done and you now have a quiet recognition of the bigger picture. This exercise to get to a mindful state can easily be done at your desk or on a lunchtime walk and is a highly effective way of recharging your energy as well as simplifying the seeming complexity of all your to-dos. Lifting your consciousness enables you to see beyond the noise and appreciate the big picture. The sun will come up tomorrow. No matter how stressed you may be or how affected you may feel by a negative interaction, life will go on. This can be a very calming perspective, courtesy of meditation and a mindful mindset.

If new to mindfulness and meditation, check out some of the great content on the Happify YouTube channel.[22]

There are also other ways of dealing with stress and breaking the chains of negative thinking. In our highly complex, scattered, and fast-moving life, we can get trapped in negative thinking patterns, which eat at our energy and absorb our focus. We might feel bad about a negative performance review we received, or be disappointed by making a mistake with something due to juggling too many things at the same time, or feel sad because our relationships are not in a good place. Whatever the reason, with so much going on in our lives we can operate for prolonged periods in these perpetuating negative states. What many of us don't realize is that getting trapped in thinking and feeling bad can have permanent implications on both your psychological and physical well-being. It can

22 https://www.youtube.com/channel/UCZ0XvEszYoBrDzBgUKEwVEA.

even result in a higher risk of mortality. Serious stuff. But there are proven techniques for breaking out of these negative states. These tested techniques revolve around shifting your perspective and sprinkling in positive experiences during your everyday routines. These include:

- **Gratitude:** This is a big one. If you ever find yourself getting caught up in the complexity of life and are feeling a little overwhelmed, just take a five-minute timeout. Find some space where you can be alone, take a couple of slow deep breaths, and then say out loud what you are thankful for. It could be "Thank you for my beautiful wife and kids, thank you for my health, thank you for all the beauty in the world, and thank you for life." This could be directed at God, the universe, or whatever you believe in. But once you start saying thank you, you will immediately feel better and all the small stuff that is weighing on you won't feel as important anymore.

- **Noticing and savoring positive events:** When you become more mindful you'll start to notice little details around you that you used to be too busy and enveloped in your own mind to see. These little details or events can give you great little shots of positivity. It could be that you notice the intricate shape of the branches in the trees on your way to work. It could be that when you open the shades first thing in the morning you pause for a couple of seconds and really enjoy the incredible colors of dawn. When something positive happens, take time to soak on it. We humans have a natural tendency to be skeptical anytime we receive positive recognition or when something good happens. Unfortunately, in instances where we could be super chuffed at receiving praise, we commonly turn it around and find a way to actually feel negative about the situation. But if we take the time to actually digest the great event, whether it be positive recognition or something else, we can let ourselves feel good, and doing this will help us break away from repetitive negativity.

- **Positive reappraisal and reframing:** Perception is reality—ain't that the truth? Every day we have a choice about how we see the world and the events that unravel around us. When we're tired, stressed, or generally frazzled it can be hard to see the good all around us. We find the negative in everything that happens to us, thereby reinforcing our negative spiral. Instead, try intentionally looking for the positive in everyday situations. See potentially terrible experiences, like dealing with conflict, making mistakes, or not getting something you want, as opportunities to learn and improve. See missing the train as an opportunity to have a five-minute meditation or enjoy the scenery where you are. This slight adjustment of perspective, or reappraisal and reframing, will help you release some of the worry and concern and get back to feeling good.

- **Setting and working toward attainable goals:** It feels good to achieve goals. It also feels good to work hard toward achieving a goal. Without goals we can lose touch of our purpose and meaning, which can make us feel a little lost and lead to depression. Setting goals gives us direction, and we are energized by the opportunity. But it is important that the goals are attainable, otherwise you'll get frustrated, give up, and then likely feel disappointed in your abilities. So, set attainable goals so that you can experience that euphoric feeling when you finally achieve the goal you worked so hard for.

- **Acts of kindness:** When your energy levels are low or you're feeling overly stressed, try giving someone a compliment or doing something nice for someone. Maybe one of your colleagues has a new haircut that you could call out, or you could simply say good morning and smile when you pass a stranger on the street. These little acts of kindness will give you a shot of positivity and break any negative funk you may have been battling to escape from.

Practicing these techniques can literally rewire your brain to not hold on to the negative and be more primed for positive experiences. It will make it more natural and easy to see all the good stuff in this world and break free from the chains of negativity, thereby lifting your energy and happiness. Stress is a natural byproduct of our fast-paced life, but with a mindful perspective and positivity tricks up your sleeve you can take more control of your mental state and energy levels.

Sleep cannot be discounted as another critical ingredient in managing energy. When we are overly stressed or cannot switch off from work, it can be difficult to get quality sleep. And when we get a bad night's sleep it directly impacts our ability to concentrate for extended periods, thereby impacting our productivity and performance. Bad sleep can create a vicious cycle: not enough sleep can fuel conflicts and result in reduced productivity, which then occupies our mind when attempting to sleep, and so on and so on. Recent scientific research has also illuminated some important biological implications of not having enough quality sleep. Our brains need deep sleep to remove toxins that build up during the day. Without deep sleep, the brain cannot clean out all the toxins and our brain can be permanently damaged, leading to the onset of Alzheimer's and other memory conditions. I am often awakened by my two young children in the middle of the night for various reasons. If this happens on consecutive nights I can feel my IQ dropping. I am significantly less productive and cannot retain concentration on anything for any extended period of time. With these experiences and all the research now available on the importance of sleep, I have become a bit of a sleep guru. I have found that there are few things that can enhance sleep:

- **Meditation:** Start repeating your mantra, because meditation is a great way of releasing all of the annoyances and concerns you may be bottling up. Taking five minutes before lights go out to sink into a meditative state effectively quiets the mind and lifts any anxiety you may have, thereby enabling you to slip into a wonderful deep sleep.

- **Limit alcohol consumption:** My sleep is significantly impacted if I have a couple of glasses of wine or beer. I may be able to go to sleep easily enough, but I wake up in the middle of the night and can't get back to sleep. Alcohol is a stimulant that affects your body in several phases. When first consumed, alcohol acts as stimulant, but then after the alcohol has been in your system for a period it acts as a sedative. Then a second stimulant phase kicks in and keeps you awake for an extended period of time.

- **Limit screen time:** Being on a screen, reading an article or watching a show, stimulates the brain's electrical activity, which diverts you from calming down into a peaceful state of mind for sleep. Also, too much light from the screen can limit the melatonin your body produces, which regulates the sleep-wake cycle, and so can make it more challenging to fall asleep.
- **No emailing or texting:** The act of responding to an email or text creates tension in your body, which can result in the stress hormone cortisol being released. This state is not conducive to sleep.

Exercise is the fourth leg to the energy management stool. Sitting is the new smoking. People are increasingly stationary in their occupations. They drive to work and then sit at their desk and tap away on their computer until it is time to hop back in their car. What many don't realize is that we often have our best revelations or epiphanies when we are going for a walk or jog. While exercising, our minds can digest and process everything we have been exposed to during the day and often make connections that were elusive when sitting at a desk putting pressure on ourselves to innovate. I remember seeing on TV some years ago that the then Australian Prime Minister John Howard takes an early morning walk every day. What a great daily routine to get your body in shape but also to gain clarity on the day's priorities. A walk after lunch is also great strategy for helping with the digestive process and reenergizing yourself without the requirement of a double espresso. I often find that if I'm struggling to get the creative juices flowing or just generally feeling unproductive, going for a run seems to do the trick. It releases tension and frustration and releases endorphins, which combine to help get my mojo back.

Energy needs to be deliberately managed and nurtured if we are to manage daily complexity and lift our innovative and productive capacity. Learning to meditate, practicing positivity, prioritizing quality sleep, and being disciplined about keeping active are great strategies for keeping our energy cranking.

In this day and age not only is there a huge opportunity to simplify organizations but the opportunity to simplify at the individual level is also significant. By decluttering, getting clear on what's truly important, planning effectively, reducing distractions and interruptions, better managing email and meetings, and nurturing and protecting energy you can build the skills and discipline to simplify your world, get a handle on complexity, and take control of your productive capacity. While each component has been somewhat skimmed over in this chapter out of necessity, our smart habits training program goes into each of these categories in much more detail and provides exercises to nurture the habits. Check our site for more information: www.simplifywork.com.

CHAPTER 5

Your Invitation to Simplify Work

Organizations of all shapes and sizes have an incredible opportunity to take a step back and look at their business through the lens of simplicity. Take a clean sheet of paper and redesign how your organization delivers value. Choose to crush all those things in your organization that are causing confusion, wasting time, and holding people back from performing at their best. This is your invitation to simplify work.

Simplifying work has to be a high priority for organizations that have become weighed down with complexity and are looking to rev up their business. It can also be a priority for those organizations that are already performing admirably but want to discover new ways of enhancing productivity, innovation, and engagement.

Every industry is now up for grabs as technology giants look to move in. Amazon is coming after everything. The time is now gone when people can come into work, blindly follow instructions, go through the motions of their repeatable processes, and play desk zombie. In this digital era, for companies to stay relevant and competitive, they require innovation and speed. Innovation and speed are bred in environments where there is crystal clarity on strategy and there is space for people to think, collaborate, experiment, and learn. Convoluted strategies; initiative overload; and controlling, debilitating, and exhausting processes, rules, and systems cannot exist in this environment.

The fourth industrial revolution that is upon us will continue to present incredible opportunities to simplify work. All repeatable and transactional tasks can finally be handed over to cloud-based software programs, thereby freeing humans to focus on more productive and higher-value work. Data collection and analytics will seamlessly occur in real time, providing a constant feed of key competitive, consumer, and market insights that can fuel rapid decision making, innovation, and execution. If we take advantage of the opportunities that emerging technologies are presenting while simplifying internal structures, processes, and ways of working, we can begin to realize the significant productivity improvements that previous industrial revolutions have delivered.

But the opportunity to simplify is not limited to organizations. There is also a substantial opportunity for individuals. Today more than ever, individuals feel overwhelmed by the number of demands on their time and attention. We work in trendy open plan offices where we are constantly interrupted. We expend time and energy on low-value-added administrative, HR, and compliance requirements. We have to waste time adhering to archaic predefined processes and rules that just get in the way of the activities that matter. There is also more work to do due to significant cost-cutting efforts. Global teams and smartphones foster an always-on mentality, which limits downtime and the ability to truly disconnect from work. This is leading to low corporate engagement rates, burnout, and turnover of talent. It also is encouraging a more reactive way of working. People jump from one fire to the next and lose sight of what is most important.

But there are some ways of simplifying work both for organizations and for individuals. It starts with leveraging the problem-solving method coming out of the field of design. Design thinking, the problem-solving method that designers use, reveals highly innovative solutions that traditional analytical problem solving does not. There are many distinctions between design thinking and typical management consulting problem solving methods. Design thinking is more human oriented, more participative, and more iterative. These characteristics are infused into a multistage method that we have reduced to three core steps to simplify work:

1. **Empathize and illuminate:** Reveal the intricacies of how work gets done today through carefully crafted questions. Lean into the richness of the experiences and probe for more color with quality questioning. Instead of just crunching numbers, the focus is on immersing oneself into the world of the user. Consider the experiences they have and ponder what is getting in the way of peak performance or what could be in place to unleash peak performance. This is a very human-

oriented way of understanding a current state and revealing key problems to solve.

2. **Ideate:** Do not simply focus on one problem to solve; take into consideration all of the challenges and opportunities and explore solutions that target a root cause. Expansively brainstorm all ideas on how to reduce and remove those things that take up too much time, cause confusion, waste energy, and get in the way of peak performance. Once diverging brainstorming is complete, converge on the few top opportunities.

3. **Prototype and implement:** Rapidly build and test the top solution ideas. Capture feedback and incorporate input to enhance the solution. Once implementation has been completed ensure that feedback channels are established to promote ongoing refinement of simplification solutions.

This method reveals creative ways of releasing capacity, increasing focus, and removing stupid rules and unnecessary time sucks. There are, however, some common areas of an organization that are sources of debilitating complexity. Having an understanding of the top triggers of complexity is very helpful when stepping into the simplification process. Using the design thinking method for targeting simplification, with the knowledge of the common drivers, helps to speed the process of sustainability simplifying your business. Here are the common drivers of complexity within organizations:

- **Unclear or scattered strategy:** Organizations that have expanded into various businesses and have a presence in a diverse set of product segments and service areas often struggle with strategic clarity. What the company truly stands for and what it is that makes the company great becomes foggy. A lack of strategic clarity disables prioritization, pulls resources too thin, and leads to reactive complacency. People gravitate to their immediate teams and lose touch of what is important at the company level.

- **Outdated organization structure:** Many of the issues that have been discussed in this book have emerged from how organizations have chosen to deal with complexity. They have used an outdated, obsolete 20th-century organization design method to cope with an expanding business. More vertical lines and boxes are added as an organization grows. With the expanding vertical structure come more processes and rules that seek to control and limit people's freedom to think and create. Organizations are left with a cobweb of roles and responsibilities and coordinating groups that essentially create too much unnecessary, low-value-added busywork.

- **Proliferating bureaucratic practices:** Bureaucratic practices squander intelligence and creativity. Unwieldy process steps and paperwork and unintelligible rules serve to aggravate and exhaust people. While they can mitigate the risk of mistakes, they also prohibit innovation and peak performance.

- **Confusing tapestry of systems:** The plethora of new software programs and applications becoming available almost weekly can create significant complexity for organizations. It can result in people needing to navigate through four systems to get their work done and decipher a labyrinth of folder structures and online repositories to find the information that is needed.

- **Counterproductive cultural habits:** People can get trapped in ways of working that waste time, limit innovation, and slow execution. These cultural traits often come to life in the form of multiple approval processes, excessive low-value meetings, email overload, and rampant overanalysis.

These common sources of organizational complexity are frequent targets for simplification efforts. Leveraging the design thinking method exposes creative ways of redesigning and/ or removing the various drivers of complexity. But the design thinking method can also reveal how to help individuals deal with personal complexity. Common solutions for individuals that feel overwhelmed in today's complex and overly complicated world include:

- **Decluttering:** Consumerism culture is pervasive and addictive. We have overcluttered our lives with too much stuff. We retain far too many things that we don't get value from. All of these things weigh on us and contribute to a sense of loss of control. Systematically reducing all the things that clutter our lives, such as excess paper, books, and clothing, delivers a sense of liberation, clarity, and focus—the gifts that simplicity offers.
- **Getting clear on what's truly important:** Having too much work, being pulled in multiple directions, and dealing with the constant stream of emails and information has led to the rise of reactive busywork. The temptation to respond to day-to-day crises and

keeping up with email and meeting requests inhibits one's ability to retain focus on those things that matter most. Regaining clarity on what's truly important, both professionally and personally, can redirect work and focus so that one becomes more proactive, impactful, and fulfilled.

- **Planning effectively:** Clarity on priorities informs the planning process. Effective planning will support the realization of priorities through translating the goals into time-bound deadlines and critical activities. An effective structure for breaking down the levels of planning is annually, quarterly, and weekly.

- **Reducing distractions and interruptions:** New emails, text messages, app updates, meeting requests, and the latest news or sports updates all provide distractions and interruptions that break our focus and get in the way of our productivity. Developing a system for managing disruptions and interruptions can help you stay focused on your highest priorities.

- **Managing email and meetings:** Email overload and low-value, time-consuming meetings eat up too much of people's time. Allocating specific times to deal with email and having a "one touch = one action" policy will free up time to focus on important matters and will break the incessant reactivity that many of us possess. Resetting expectations on who should be included on emails can help to reduce the quantity of emails received. Also, simply having the confidence to say no to low-value meetings or suggesting a reduction in the meeting timeframe not only can free up productive time but also can foster an effective meeting culture.

- **Nurturing and protecting energy:** There is generally a lack of acknowledgment of the importance of nurturing and protecting personal energy. There is not enough recognition of people's most productive times and being deliberate with protecting that time for the most important work. Also, more can be done to help people to effectively maintain and recharge energy levels. Building skills in mindfulness practices like meditation can have a great effect on managing energy levels. So can enhancing the quality of sleep and building habits around frequent exercise.

The act of simplification can be a tremendously liberating exercise for both organizations and individuals. But it takes confidence and commitment to really tap into the power of simplification. Without dedication and discipline, it becomes too easy to fall back into old routines and habits. The temptation to check that email, respond to the latest fire, or attend the meeting just because you've been invited will be great. The command-and-control management style that has become second nature in many organizations will want to rear its head, but you can't let it. Giving people the space to think, innovate, fail, and learn is always very difficult for leaders. It's like teaching your child to swim: there comes a point where you have to let go and trust they will be able to cope without you. Thankfully, the mentality of leaders is changing and there is rising recognition that to get the best out of people you have to give them autonomy—but autonomy with clear direction and guidelines to work within. The path to simplification requires perseverance, but it will deliver tremendous results if you stick with it. And it is a path that will become an inevitable one for any organization that desires longevity.

Imagine...

Imagine how work would look if simplification took hold. Imagine walking down the halls of your company and feeling the energy emanating from team rooms. Imagine witnessing your people so excited by the hot project they're working on that they can't wait to jump into problem solving with their team members. You witness teams going for walks or taking their project work outside, and you can't help but see the smiles and enthusiasm for work that exudes from each individual. All of a sudden you realize that you're on a winning team, and you and your teams are delivering impact and it feels good.

Creating this environment is possible, and many companies have achieved it. It all starts with letting simplification provide the guiding light for how your company should operate. And it is incredible how simplification will take hold. It's like releasing a cap on a pressure valve. Imagine the surge in innovation and productivity that would be realized by people having the space and time to think, innovate, and execute. Imagine the spike in employee engagement that would occur with people spending more time on the work they were hired to do and being able to achieve more balance between their professional and personal lives. A workforce that is healthier has more energy, more focus, and delivers more impact on the business, and you can imagine how organizations would finally be able to tap into the potential of their workforce. The time is right to liberate the best in all of us through simplifying work.

With the rise of technological capabilities, the opportunities to simplify work will accelerate. Imagine if all time-consuming and energy-sapping activities were automated. What if booking flights was as easy as telling a robotic voice assistant your flight destination and preferred times? The robot assistant would then quickly analyze flight options as well as hotels at the destination, incorporating travel policies and reviewing your calendar, and complete the booking. Once the travel is completed, the robotic assistant would process all expenses by pulling all transactions from your credit card that occurred during the travel period and automatically submitting them to the appropriate system for processing. What if there was one system that morphed together your online community, learning opportunities, corporate communications, performance management, and documentation repository and provided real-time insights into the company's performance? What if this same single platform also captured your health? What if your health vitals were constantly recorded, analyzed, and displayed on this same home page? Employees would be informed when their energy levels are low or stress levels too high and encouraged to take a 10-minute meditation break. This one platform could also obviously be accessed on any device and could be easily switched off when you need to focus on a particular document or task.

Let's take it a step further. Imagine if in this future state where simplification has taken hold, many back-office functions have automated all repeatable processes. Humans are only engaged on strategically important activities. The types of activities that are automated across these functions could include:

- Finance
  - Recording all transactions

- Completing all financial reporting, both internal and external
- Closing the books
- Setting and monitoring budgets
- Managing all accounts receivable and payable
- Providing real-time financial positions
• Human resources
  - Automating recruitment
  - Enabling ongoing simple and insightful performance management
  - Managing all payroll and benefits, including executive compensation
  - Providing real-time employee engagement insights
• Supply chain
  - Automating all procurement
  - Managing warehousing and inventory
  - Monitoring and managing all distribution

The roles that would be left in these functions would be focused on extrapolating insight from the current performance of the function and uncovering opportunities for further enhancing performance. With these back-office functions automated, the structure of the rest of the organization is designed so that small teams have the freedom to go after the biggest opportunities. These opportunities are organized in logical pods or groupings and are coordinated by floating groups that connect in informal and non-time-consuming ways. People are freed and enabled to spend their best time and energy on the highest-value work in an environment that fosters and stimulates rich collaboration, intellectual exploration, and experimentation.

Imagine what work would feel like if there were no power plays or hallway politics. Imagine if everyone were given the opportunity to add value. Imagine how people would blossom when not controlled by three managers. Furthermore, there would be no more managers doing nothing and taking credit for their team's hard work. There would be significantly less waste: less wasted time on low-value, nonsensical activities or processes, and less waste from stripping out all the non-value-adding roles, committees, and coordinating functions. All of this significant reduction in waste has one really big and important implication: lower costs. Leaders will take notice of this one.

However, while there would be great productivity enhancements and cost savings by simplifying work, there would also be areas requiring some investment. Those people transitioning out of roles that traditionally managed repeatable processes will need to learn new skills. If the expectation is that humans now operate in roles where they deliver value and any role that can be defined by standards and processes be automated, then many individuals will need to build new capabilities. In particular, key capabilities required in this new world include:

- Problem solving
- Information synthesis
- Effective teamworking
- Project management
- Intellectual curiosity and expansive thinking

These are not easy capabilities to build, so carefully constructed learning programs will need to be built to effectively facilitate this development journey, which will require some investment.

In today's digital environment, some organizations are leading the way and have freed their people to do their best work, but many are being left behind. They are held back by crippling risk aversion or are paralyzed by the scale of their embedded complexity. But I encourage you to take the first step. Leverage the design thinking method and lean into the reality of how work is done in your organization to uncover the simplicity bottlenecks. You may find that one or many of the following levers need to be pulled:

- Simplifying strategy
- Rethinking structure
- Stripping out bureaucratic practices
- Making sense of systems
- Removing counterproductive cultural traits

Simplifying work can be done with strong and unwavering leadership commitment. As the speed of industry evolution accelerates, those organizations that are bogged down in complexity may lose the opportunity to turn their business around or counter the threat from fast-moving technology companies.

The image of what work could be like when simplification takes hold is an inspiring one. The idea of people rapidly learning and developing, using all of their creative potential, and positively throwing all of their energy into work that matters is a beautiful image. I think we can get there. We just have to start with this vision and then take the first step to simplify work.

This is your invitation to simplify work.

If you would like to assess what is getting in the way of top performance at your organization then I encourage you to utilize the free Simplify Work complexity assessment at www.simplifywork.com. Feel free to also reach out to us at hi@ simplifywork.com if you would like to discuss your organization in more detail.

ACKNOWLEDGMENTS

First and foremost I would to thank my wife, Kelly, for encouraging me to take this journey. She was sitting next to me by that campfire in the Serengeti and helped stoke the fire within me to take this on. Her ongoing support, guidance, and encouragement has really helped me cross the finish line. Thank you.

Special thanks go to Barton Tretheway, who immediately offered guidance and support when I first raised the idea of writing a book while barbequing on a beautiful late fall evening in Chicago. Thank you, Barton, for not only reviewing and providing great feedback on my content, but also for introducing me to a set of individuals that provided guidance that would shape my book writing journey.

A big thank-you to the experienced authors that agreed to meet with me and share their guidance and insights:

- Tom Kuczmarski

- Scott Davis
- Bill Welter
- BK Simerson

It's been a privilege to work with Lori Paximadis, my editor. Her eye for detail and honest feedback really polished this book. I have learned a lot from your feedback and I thank you for your partnership.

Thanks to David Hancock and the team at Morgan James Publishing. Your fun and easy approach to publishing has been greatly appreciated.

Finally, I'd like to thank my parents, Rowena Robinson and John Newton. Thank you for all of the sacrifices you made to give me opportunities to flourish. Your unwavering love and belief in me is felt and deeply recognized.

ABOUT THE AUTHOR

Jesse W. Newton is the founder and CEO of Simplify Work, a global consultancy that specializes in unburdening organizations from paralyzing complexity (www.simplify-work.com). In his work with clients, Newton advises across the spectrum of simplification focal areas, including rethinking organizational structure, transforming culture, and building smart skills in individuals and teams. Clients include Mondelez International, McDonald's Corporation, and PepsiCo.

Prior to launching Simplify Work, Newton was a senior member of Booz & Company's Organization, Change and Leadership consulting practice. He also spent a number of years consulting with Ernst & Young's People & Organizational Change practice.

As an expert advisor in Northwestern University's postgraduate Designing for Organization Effectiveness Certification (DOEC) program, Newton provides practical coaching and is a speaker on topics including organization design, culture, and talent management.

Newton is the author of "Three Secrets of Organization Effectiveness," published in *Strategy + Business* (volume 76, autumn 2014). He is also an international speaker and frequently appears in various news publications on the topic of organizational simplification.

Newton received his master of science degree in learning and organizational change from Northwestern University and a bachelor of commerce degree from Victoria University of Wellington with first class honors in management and international business.

Newton is a proud husband and father of two beautiful girls. He spends his time between homes in Chicago, Illinois, and Big Sky, Montana.